Alice Walker and Zora Neale Hurston

Recent Titles in
Contributions in Afro-American and African Studies

The Racial Problem in the Works of Richard Wright and James Baldwin
Jean-François Gounard; Joseph J. Rodgers, Jr., translator

Renaissance Man from Louisiana: A Biography of Arna Wendell Bontemps
Kirkland C. Jones

A Struggle Worthy of Note: The Engineering and Technological Education
David E. Wharton

African American Soldiers in the National Guard: Recruitment and Deployment During Peacetime and War
Charles Johnson, Jr.

Religion and Suicide in the African-American Community
Kevin E. Early

State Against Development: The Experience of Post-1965 Zaire
Mondonga M. Mokoli

Dusky Maidens: The Odyssey of the Early Black Dramatic Actress
Jo A. Tanner

Language and Literature in the African American Imagination
Carol Aisha Blackshire-Belay, editor

Visible Ellison: A Study of Ralph Ellison's Fiction
Edith Schor

The Early Black Press in America, 1827 to 1860
Frankie Hutton

The Black Laws in the Old Northwest: A Documentary History
Stephen Middleton

The African Aesthetic: Keeper of the Traditions
Kariamu Welsh-Asante, editor

History and Hunger in West Africa: Food Production and Entitlement in Guinea-Bissau and Cape Verde
Laura Bigman

Financing Health Care in Sub-Saharan Africa
Ronald J. Vogel

Folk Wisdom and Mother Wit: John Lee—An African American Herbal Healer
Arvilla Payne-Jackson and John Lee; Illustrations by Linda Kempton Armstrong

Alice Walker and Zora Neale Hurston

THE COMMON BOND

Edited by Lillie P. Howard

Contributions in Afro-American and African Studies, Number 163

Greenwood Press
Westport, Connecticut • London

Library of Congress Cataloging-in-Publication Data

Alice Walker and Zora Neale Hurston : the common bond / edited by Lillie P. Howard.
p. cm. — (Contributions in Afro-American and African studies, ISSN 0069-9624 ; no. 163)
Includes bibliographical references and index.
ISBN 0-313-25790-6 (alk. paper)
1. American fiction—Afro-American authors—History and criticism. 2. American fiction—Women authors—History and criticism. 3. American fiction—20th century—History and criticism. 4. Walker, Alice, 1944- —Criticism and interpretation. 5. Hurston, Zora Neale—Criticism and interpretation. 6. Afro-American women in literature. 7. Afro-Americans in literature. I. Howard, Lillie P. II. Series.
PS374.N4A44 1993
813'.5099287—dc20 93-20324

British Library Cataloguing in Publication Data is available.

Library of Congress Catalog Card Number: 93-20324
ISBN: 0-313-25790-6
ISSN: 0069-9624

First published in 1993

Greenwood Press, 88 Post Road West, Westport, CT 06881
An imprint of Greenwood Publishing Group, Inc.

Printed in the United States of America

The paper used in this book complies with the Permanent Paper Standard issued by the National Information Standards Organization (Z39.48-1984).

10 9 8 7 6 5 4 3 2

95 0969

To Kimberly and Benjamin Kendricks, my children,
who brought into my life the precious gift of themselves
and
To my mother, Zola Mae Howard,
who died (in December 1987) without ever telling me her story
or realizing that she should.

Contents

Preface

> When I sit down in order to write, sometimes it's there; sometimes it's not. . . . There is such a thing as "writer's block," and [you] should respect it. You shouldn't write through it. It's blocked because it ought to be blocked, because you haven't got it right now. All the frustration and nuttiness that comes from "Oh, my God, I cannot write now" should be displaced. It's just a message to you saying, "That's right, you can't write now, so don't." . . . If I don't have anything to say for three or four months, I just don't write. When I read a book, I can always tell if the writer has written through a block. If he or she had waited, it would have been better or different, or a little more natural. You can see the seams.
>
> —Toni Morrison in Tate, *Black Women Writers at Work* (120)

The idea of writing a book on Alice Walker and Zora Neale Hurston came to me approximately ten years ago, but like Hurston with her first novel, *Jonah's Gourd Vine*, I hid the idea away in the light of day but grappled with it at night, feeling that perhaps it was too big for me to attempt, that surely someone else was already about it, that my time might be better spent writing more about Zora, leaving Alice alone and simply waiting for the book to emerge from the efforts of others.

Ten years ago I went so far as to write a multipage essay exploring similarities between the two writers, and sent it to a journal that, I learned a few weeks later, had gone out of business; I got it back by return mail with a note to that effect, resignedly tucked the manuscript away in a box, and that was that. Or so I thought. But the idea would not go away, particularly as African-American literature scholars and even casual readers of Hurston and Walker continued to note that the two writers were remarkably alike though, until recently, few ventured to offer details beyond that observation.

So, to still my inner discontent, I began in 1985 to assemble a gallery of contributors to give the Walker/Hurston idea a fair hearing. The contributors' enthusiasm fed my own; I secured a contract with Greenwood Press, and the project was launched. Then, almost immediately, the time I thought I would have to work on the book disappeared. Instead, life took over, leaving in its wake the vagaries, challenges, and inevitable bereavements of day-to-day existence. When some of the contributors to the book were similarly beset, I became content to wait. Rather than brooding and throwing up my hands, I became a student of the process of writing itself, the process of trying to find the time to create when your life is not your own. Thus, seeking solace, I found it in Toni Morrison who had said in her interview with Claudia Tate in *Black Women Writers at Work* that sometimes you simply have to wait. Indeed, it is better that you do. . . .

I thought often, of course, of our foremothers, forging a way out of no way, planting their flowers in stolen moments of serenity, quilting their art out of love and necessity. Soon a kind of mental lethargy set in, hounding my days and nights, grabbing hold like Coleridge's albatross, sucking enjoyment out of life. I was caught between a book that would "out" and the widening gyre of the ever-present, ever-demanding moment. No doubt sensing my dilemma, Alice Walker published another novel, not *Olive Oil*, as many of us had been led to expect after *The Color Purple*, but the maddening *The Temple of My Familiar*. What better way to finish a book quickly (long in the making) than to be confronted with another Walker novel, this one spanning all of time? I could hardly ignore it, so, of course, I plunged right in, again and again. Meantime, Walker also published *Her Blue Body* (a collection of her poetry) and another novel, *Possessing the Secret of Joy*. And through that process of waiting, inching along, and retreating through time with *The Temple* and then beginning anew with each subsequent Walker publication, *The Common Bond* was finally born.

~

Judging by the number of works that have been published on Walker and Hurston during the past five years, a number of other scholars of African-American literature have also been exploring the Hurston-Walker connection, variously interpreting and defining that bond, broadening our understanding of the two writers, of African-American literature and theory in general. Henry Louis Gates, Jr.'s *The Signifying Monkey* (1985) and *Reading Black, Reading Feminist* (1990), Melvin Dixon's *Ride Out the Wilderness: Geography and Identity in Afro-American Literature* (1987), Calvin Hernton's *The Sexual Mountain and Black Women*

Writers (1987), Joanne Braxton and Andree Nicola McLaughlin's *Wild Women in the Whirlwind* (1990), Susan Willis's *Specifying: Black Women Writing the American Experience*, and Marjorie Pryse and Hortense Spillers's *Conjuring* (1985) all, to varying degrees, explore the Hurston-Walker bond. Essayists Molly Hite, Trudy Bloser Bush, Sabine Brock, and Anne Koenen also offer commentary, tightening the Hurston-Walker knot. Together, all of these writers suggest that the connection is compelling, spiritual, literary, haunting, comforting, timeless, and adequate grist for our literary mills.

Still, in spite of all of our efforts, Alice Walker and Zora Neale Hurston remain pretty much in bas-relief. It is as though their words, their images, take on a life of their own, with Zora and Alice remaining hidden behind a facade of their and perhaps our making. During the past two decades, both writers have become shrouded in legend, in stories, real and imagined, meant to illuminate who they are. While critics, observers, truth- and nay-sayers continue to hold forth on both writers, Hurston and Walker seem to move a piece on down their own roads, keeping a step or two beyond our grasp. With each new work, Alice Walker simultaneously expands her definition of who she is and erases it, *The Temple of My Familiar* being a tantalizing example. And, of course, we are still missing ten years of Zora's life. Either we need to admit that she was simply ten years older than we thought when she finished high school, entered Barnard College, published *Their Eyes Were Watching God* (at forty-six), and so on, or we need to get busy filling in what appears to be an enormous gap. It is better to admit immediately, then, the limitations of this book rather than to pretend, in the interest of the "truth," that we have finally unearthed all of it. What I said in 1980 in my book on Zora (called simply, *Zora Neale Hurston*), then, applies not only to Zora but to Alice Walker as well:

> For the past few years, students, critics, and friends have tried to fathom the enigma known as Zora Neale Hurston. They will continue to probe her mystery but I am convinced that no one will ever produce a definitive Zora Hurston. The best one can hope for is a reasonable facsimile thereof, a superior piecing together of all the parts, the evidence. But one must always remember that evidence sometimes lies (especially since Zora herself, the provider of the evidence, often lied), that even when it does not lie, it must be interpreted, that interpretations, governed as they are by the nature and limitations of our own experiences, are subjective, that our images of Zora Neale Hurston will always be just that—ours. (Howard 7)

In many ways, both Zora and Alice are a million Miss Lissies (a character in *The Temple)* with many of their multiple lives still hidden, still left untold. All we really know about these two writers, then, as Zora hints in her "autobiography," *Dust Tracks*, is that they did "get born" (though now that we know *when* for Zora, we still do not know exactly *where* since Alabama holds as strong a possibility for place of birth as Eatonville, Florida). We also know that, between them, they have published a number of impressive essays, short stories, novels, other books, volumes of poetry, and won a number of impressive awards—fellowships, the Pulitzer Prize, and American Book Award, to name a few, for Walker; the Anisfield-Wolf Award and Guggenheim fellowships aplenty for Zora. All the rest is hearsay. So, we take it for what it is, a sorry substitute for the real thing, and we begin to fashion something like what follows. When all is said and done, it is the best we can do, and for all we know, it may actually be better than the real thing.

~

Like both Walker and Hurston, *The Common Bond* is itself unorthodox and will thus not fit the mold many of us have been trained to expect in literary criticism. While, as you will see later, some of this is intentional, much of it is not. When I learned from Walker's publisher, Harcourt Brace Jovanovich, that after extraordinary effort on my and the publisher's part, Alice Walker and thus Harcourt Brace Jovanovich had denied my request to use excerpts from her writings in my book—excerpts that had appeared in each contributor's essay—I was not crestfallen. The publisher had told me at the outset that Walker had a policy not to have excerpts from her works reproduced. One could reproduce an entire work (after paying the requisite permission fee), but one could not simply quote a few lines. No doubt from Walker's viewpoint, disallowing excerpts would reduce the opportunity for misunderstanding, misinterpretation, and questionable but highly negative criticism of the sort that has haunted the public's reception of some of her writings. All that, I understood and respected. Still, I asked the publisher to see if Walker would make an exception given the scholarly nature of the work. The publisher asked, Walker refused, and so here we are.

I do not despair. Rather, I am determined to play the hand I have been dealt, to go betwixt since I cannot go between, to present to the public a book that will rely upon the individual will and memory of each reader to supply the evidence, to read between the lines, to fill the white spaces with the appropriate passages remembered from their own readings of Walker's works. This book, stripped of many of those passages we as scholars have come to rely upon as good scholarly practice, then, relies for its success upon the active participation, the appropriate response, of a community of scholars/readers.

~

The essays in *The Common Bond* cover a broad spectrum, from folklore and spirituality in the works of Walker and Hurston to liberation of the self, regardless of gender. They cover much of the fiction of both writers, most often their most compelling works—Hurston's *Their Eyes Were Watching God* and Walker's *The Color Purple*—but also Walker's *The Third Life of Grange Copeland*; *In Love and Trouble*; *Meridian*; *The Temple of My Familiar*; and *Possessing the Secret of Joy*; and Hurston's *Jonah's Gourd Vine*; *Mules and Men* (collection of folklore); *Moses, Man of the Mountain*; and *Dust Tracks on a Road*.

In "Zora Neale Hurston: A Cautionary Tale and a Partisan View" (reprinted in full here with the publisher's permission), Alice Walker says that in her mind,

> Zora Neale Hurston, Billie Holiday, and Bessie Smith form a sort of unholy trinity. Zora *belongs* in the tradition of black women singers, rather than among "the literati." . . . Like Billie and Bessie she followed her own road, believed in her own gods, pursued her own dreams, and refused to separate herself from "common people."

The essay offers a nice tribute to Hurston, a libation of sorts which Walker continues to offer to Hurston in subsequent essays and books.

In "Settling the Dust: Tracking Zora Through Alice Walker's 'The Revenge of Hannah Kemhuff,' " Mary L. Navarro and Mary H. Sims establish Walker's first literary link with Zora, a link that not only fictionalizes (i.e., turns into a story) Walker's mother's experiences but Walker's literary bond with Hurston as well. The evidence these two authors offer is compelling and affirming.

In "Our People, Our People," Trudier Harris points out that "not only do these two authors use folklore in their fiction, but they themselves have become subjects of African-American folklore. Stories float about them as readily as they do about some of the characters they created." Harris adds: "Both of these women writers . . . have been claimed by the very folk traditions that have served as inspiration to their creative endeavors; they provide striking examples of the strength of African-American folk culture as process and as art."

In "A Sense of Wonder: The Pattern for Psychic Survival in *Their Eyes Were Watching God* and *The Color Purple*," Alice Fannin explores similarities between Janie and Celie, concluding that "for each woman, then, psychic survival depends . . . not so much on greater self-awareness and independence . . . but on the vision of the self as a wondrous part of a Creation that is itself 'wondrously and fearfully' made."

In " 'That Which the Soul Lives By': Spirituality in the Works of Zora Neale Hurston and Alice Walker," Mary Ann Wilson suggests that Hurston and Walker's works give us "characters who not only embrace their culture as a source of strength but also transcend it by creating an alternative reality either of language or action," or both, one leading to the other, and both emerging out of the culture itself.

Emma J. Waters Dawson points out, in "Redemption Through Redemption of the Self in *Their Eyes Were Watching God* and *The Color Purple*" that the female protagonists in *Their Eyes* and *Color Purple* survive suffering by re-creating themselves, realizing their artistic potential, and drawing encouragement from a network of women with whom they share their experiences.

Valerie Babb, in "Women and Words: Articulating the Self in *Their Eyes Were Watching God* and *The Color Purple*," continues to look at these two authors' female characters, explaining that "in both works . . . it is access to words that allows all of the women characters to find themselves and then place themselves in larger social and cultural contexts." In both *Their Eyes* and *Color Purple*, says Babb, "not only do we have the personal development of women illustrated through a growing facility with words, we also have the importance of the word in African-American culture documented and memorialized."

None of this is surprising, suggests JoAnne Cornwell in "Searching for Zora in Alice's Garden: Rites of Passage in Hurston's *Their Eyes Were Watching God* and Walker's *The Third Life of Grange Copeland*," for "through her sense of mission, Walker actively fulfills the legacy of Zora Neale Hurston" and exemplifies an "acute sense of being rooted in a unique feminine artistic tradition of which Zora Hurston is probably the most important precursor." According to Cornwell-Giles, Hurston's work established "the framework for the literary tradition in which Alice Walker participates." In Walker's work, we thus see "the personal, cultural, and technical aspects of African-American creative expression . . . concretized."

Ann Folwell Stanford ("Dynamics of Change: Men and Co-Feeling in the Fiction of Zora Neale Hurston and Alice Walker") links the development (or lack of it) of John Pearson of *Jonah's Gourd Vine* and Moses of *Moses, Man of the Mountain* with that of Grange of *The Third Life* and Albert of *The Color Purple*, concluding that all four men move toward "alternative modes of being and knowing where human attachment and compassion are seen as powerful factors in moral development."

In "Zora Neale Hurston and Alice Walker: A Transcendent Relationship—*Jonah's Gourd Vine* and *The Color Purple*," Ayana Karanja argues that Walker and Hurston share the same worldview because they both spent their youth in states adjacent to each other in the southeastern United States. She points out that runaway slaves from Georgia frequently found refuge in Florida, unwittingly advancing "cultural diffusion" (values assimilation between groups, exchange of language systems, etc.). Karanja further advances that Walker and Hurston's "use of the oppositional themes, vulnerability and ancient African female power, are coexistent, centripetal forces in their female protagonists' lives."

Not surprisingly, *The Color Purple* and *Their Eyes Were Watching God* come in for the most discussion here. Just what there is about these two novels that attracts the sustained attention of Hurston and Walker scholars, almost to the complete exclusion of the authors' other works, is not difficult to understand. After all, in *Their Eyes Were Watching God*, Hurston captures the journey of a lifetime, holding up in Janie's protracted struggles the struggles of us all. But because Janie meets with triumph in the end, having discovered her own independence, resiliency, and inner strength, we are nudged toward and encouraged to discover own own. And so time and time again, the contributors express appreciation for *Their Eyes*, a work that returns to us our essential, unabashed selves, and that insists that we value every whit of the collective as well as the individual cache.

Walker's *The Color Purple* replays this theme—in what Henry Louis Gates, Jr. (*The Signifying Monkey*) calls "an act of ancestral bonding that is especially rare in black letters"—setting before us a repressed Celie, articulate in her silence, compelling in her pain, exasperating, like Janie, in her patience, but nonetheless a woman who must and does discover her own power to re-create herself in her own image.

Both Janie and Celie, then, are given license, through a kind of "holy boldness," to unleash themselves, to *speak* themselves into the headiness of their own splendor. No other works by Walker or Hurston speak to us in quite this way. And so the contributors to *The Common Bond* have a great deal to say about these two works, which are inextricably yoked in their own consciousness, *The Color Purple* being the place to which Walker would inevitably arrive given Hurston as a literary model.

Put another way, most of the essays describe Janie and Celie as women who, in poet Maya Angelou's words, "survive as themselves, who find "safety and sanctity inside themselves" in order to tolerate, to transcend, to daily slough off "tortuous lives" (*I Dream a World* 8).

I make my own contributions to this book not only as editor, but also in the "Introduction," which repeats much of what we have "heard" about

Walker and Hurston, and in the concluding chapter, a "Benediction," which muses about Walker's *The Temple of My Familiar* and *Possessing the Secret of Joy*. These musings, hampered by Alice Walker's insistence that no excerpts from her texts be used, for any purpose, skim the surfaces of these two works. They primarily capture, then, this reader's experiences of the works, leaving substantial explication of the texts to another time and place when, perhaps, the rules might be different.

In addition to offering the reader a book that, in Wayne Booth's terms (*The Rhetoric of Fiction*), *tells* more than it *shows*, it will be obvious throughout that I have taken some liberty with the book, politely refusing to conform exactly to structure, doing exactly as I please on more than one occasion. I have done so in the interest of letting my own spirit soar in harmony with Zora and Alice and with each of the contributors to the book. At the same time, I have tried to personalize my contributions because I believe that both Walker and Hurston are about personalizing life, putting us all in touch with what matters most, which, when all is said and done, is simply our individual and collective selves at one with the universe. It seems somehow disrespectful, then, or even a little "ig'nant" not to let all of us have our say.

~

Heartfelt thanks to all those who have made this book possible: Alice Walker, Zora Neale Hurston, Harcourt Brace Jovanovich, the University of Illinois at Bloomington, HarperCollins, the *Zora Neale Hurston Forum*, and each of the contributors. Many thanks also to my former secretary, Judi Engle, who goodnaturedly typed much of an interim draft and then left to take another position, but who later graciously returned on Saturdays to finish up; to Patty Seifert, my current secretary, and Pam Wheeler, who pitched in at crucial moments so that I could keep moving toward the end; to my indefatigable research assistant Mai Nguyen, who plied me with every article and book she could find on the captioned subject; and to my children, Kimberly and Benjamin, who have decided that I am "the bestest mom they got," no matter what.

Finally, every now and then, I feel Zora's spirit flitting about, spurring me on to I know not what. Zora, for entering my life and staying with me all these years, I thank you. And Alice, for having the courage to save not only the life that is your own but also a multitude of others, I offer libation, and start to humming.

I

“The Call and the Response”

1

Introduction: Alice and Zora— "The Call and the Response"

Lillie P. Howard

Both Alice Walker and Zora Neale Hurston are children of the South. Both are brilliantly talented, political, controversial, receiving mixed reviews within their own communities. Both have written a number of works and both have won a slew of awards, Alice Walker becoming the first black woman novelist to win the Pulitzer Prize for fiction (for *The Color Purple*, which also won the American Book Award) and Zora winning the Anisfield-Wolf Award (for her autobiography, *Dust Tracks on a Road)* for "the best book on race relations . . . and the best volume in the general field of fiction, poetry, or biography."

Zora was born on January 7, 1891, either in the all-black town of Eatonville, Florida, or in Notasulga, Alabama (as her brother Everette claimed); Alice Walker was born fifty-three years later, on February 9, 1944, in Eatonton, Georgia. Zora was the sixth of eight children born to John Hurston and Lucy Ann Potts, Alice the last of eight children born to Willie Lee and Minnie Lou Grant. While Walker's parents were sharecroppers, with everybody in the family picking cotton for the grand sum of three hundred dollars during a good year, Zora's mother was a former school teacher, her father a carpenter, mayor of Eatonville, pastor of the local Baptist church, and moderator of the South Florida Baptist Association.

Both Zora and Alice were their mother's child, Zora looking to her mother for understanding, support, protection, and encouragement, Alice seeing her mother as an example of how one can create art out of pain, if not because of, then in defiance of it. Minnie Lou's art manifested itself not only in quilting and in the flower gardens she planted, but in the stories that she and Alice's aunts told, in their sense of self and independence, and in the assurance with which they approached life. In spite of encouragement from the women in their lives, however, neither Zora nor Alice found growing up easy or without trauma.

Zora was curious and restless, feeling the need to wander and discover things:

> I used to climb to the top of one of the huge chinaberry trees which guarded our front gate and look out over the world. The most interesting thing that I saw was the horizon. . . . It grew upon me that I ought to walk out to the horizon and see what the end of the world was like. (*Dust Tracks* 44)

Her father urged her to know her place as a "Negro," and thus to forego "white" things like dreaming and yearning for full self-expression.

When her mother died when Zora was fourteen, Zora was cast out of her home by her father, who quickly remarried. She was passed around from relative to relative, and sent for a time to join her sister and brother in school in Jacksonville, where her father offered to let the school adopt her.

Given this hand-to-mouth existence, Zora had to delay finishing high school until 1918, when she graduated from Morgan Academy, the high school division of what is now Morgan State University. From there, she attended Howard University, taking classes intermittently until 1924, studying under poet Georgia Douglas Johnson and philosopher Alain Locke, and beginning to write short stories. These stories brought her to the attention of the sociologist and shaker and mover of the Harlem Renaissance, Charles Spurgeon Johnson, who invited her to New York to try her fortune as a writer. Zora enjoyed many benefits from her experiences in New York during the Harlem Renaissance, one of these being a scholarship to Barnard College, from which she graduated in 1928, after a significant apprenticeship with famed anthropologist Franz Boas.

Alice Walker, too, needed "peace, solitude and gentle handling" (De Veaux 56) as a child. While Alice Walker did not lose a parent when she was young, like Zora she felt estranged from her father and often from her sisters and brothers: "I used to think I had just dropped into my family, and I didn't know by whom or what. I think I started writing just to keep from being so lonely, from being so much the outsider" (De Veaux 58). When at the age of eight, she lost the sight in one eye when one of her brothers shot her with a BB gun, she felt for a time estranged from the world. This estrangement, however, catapulting her into the role of the observer, gave her the ability to see better and deeper.

Graduating from high school in 1961 as valedictorian of her class and the recipient of a rehabilitation scholarship from the state of Georgia, Alice entered Spelman College in Atlanta, and, two years later, Sarah Lawrence College in Bronxville, New York. She says in *I Dream a World* that she "was forced to leave Spelman College":

> I was a rebel, without knowing or planning. I wanted to be myself and I could not do that while thinking about whether my seams were straight, and my hair was straight, and my dress was ironed, and my slip wasn't showing. The administration made it clear that if we were arrested in political demonstrations, we could be expelled. They were on the side of the system, even though we were trying to change apartheid in the South. (24)

From this school for turning black girls into ladies, Alice fled to Sarah Lawrence, where an unexpected pregnancy again turned her thoughts to suicide. Instead of killing herself, however, she discovered the staying power and healing balm of friendship and of writing poetry. With the help of a friend, she visited an abortionist, and afterward she began to write poetry, writing almost nonstop nearly all of the poems in *Once*. Walker graduated from Sarah Lawrence in 1965.

While Alice Walker began her literary career by writing poetry at Sarah Lawrence, Zora Hurston began hers by writing short stories at Howard. Both were helped along by college professors, Zora by Georgia Douglas Johnson and Alain Locke, who sent her stories on to Charles Johnson, Alice by Muriel Rukeyser, who helped her to publish *Once*.

Both Alice and Zora, after having spent some time at a black college, were shaped by the academic milieu of northern women's colleges. Alice's first publication, "The Civil Rights Movement: How Good Was It," won the *American Scholar* essay contest; Zora's short stories, "Drenched in Light" and "Spunk," and a play, *Color Struck*, won prizes sponsored by *Opportunity* magazine.

After graduating from their respective colleges, both women returned to the South, Alice to Mississippi to work along with her husband, civil rights attorney Melvyn Leventhal, in voter registration drives, Zora—first under the patronage of Franz Boas and the Carter G. Woodson Foundation, later under contract with Charlotte Osgood Mason—to Florida, Alabama, and New Orleans to collect folklore, everyday stories and lies people were passing around on the porch of the local community store (Joe Clark's porch).

In returning to the South after a stint up north, both women were in essence beginning the all-important journey toward the self, using the tools they had acquired in college to begin the task, but soon sloughing off much of that mantle in order better to immerse themselves in their blackness. For Zora, it was important to capture and preserve that spirit and reality she had witnessed during the exchanges on Joe Clark's porch:

> Men sat around the store on boxes and benches and passed this world and the next one through their mouths. The right and the wrong, the who, when and why was passed on, and nobody doubted the conclusions. There were no discreet nuances of life on Joe Clark's porch. There was open kindnesses, anger, hate, love, envy and its kinfolk, but all emotions were naked, and nakedly arrived at. It was a case of "make it and take it." You got what your strengths could bring you. (*Dust Tracks* 69–70)

These "crayon enlargements of life" would form the backdrop for much of Zora's fiction and all of her life.

Put simply, Zora wanted to exalt black people and black culture, as they were, to encourage black people to see themselves anew and be proud, to recognize the art, the rich metaphors and similes that flowed effortlessly from their lips every day, to accept and perpetuate this image of themselves in lieu of the negative images of blacks perpetuated by others, sometimes even by themselves. She wanted to tell stories about men and women, about love and hate and misunderstanding, about marriage and life and life's possibilities, about selfhood and ultimately nationhood. She did tell such stories, and she told them so well that black folks all over, and even an impressive number of white folks, have found themselves hewn out of them. She also wanted to add a woman's voice to the all-male chorus on the Eatonville store's porch—to make women participants as well as observers, co-equals, sitting beside the men and making women's meaning out of the world.

Years later what Alice Walker was to find and praise in Zora's work was its "racial health: a sense of black people as complete, complex, *undiminished* human beings, a sense that is lacking in so much black writing and literature" ("Foreword," Hemenway xviii; reprinted in this volume). According to Walker, Zora wrote down what others did not care to record or preserve, hoping by their negligence to suppress all that did not conform to white expectations. Rather than denying that which made her what she was, then—her strong, unadorned, southern roots—Zora embraced her people and her culture, allowing and encouraging those who would come after her to do the same.

"Walker's return to the South," explains Thadious Davis,

> coincides with her turning to the people, land, and customs of her childhood for the raw materials of her art. Her parents, family, and older residents of her community provide her with the starting point of her narratives, which are shaped by the rural Georgia of her youth: cotton fields, hogwire fences, sharecroppers' shacks, red clay gullies. Despite a strong sense of place, Walker's fiction is neither provincial nor dependent upon local color for significance. She evokes concrete scenes as a means of communicating the richness of a folk heritage and the presence of a tenacious will to survive. (352)

In *The Third Life of Grange Copeland*, the novel that grew out of this period, the South is just as much a character as Grange Copeland. Active, exacting, unflinching, and unyielding, the South and its ways hold sway over three generations of people until Grange Copeland, during his third life, rises to take control of his private life just as Martin Luther King, Jr. (an off-stage character in the novel) publicly does the same. Writes Davis:

> Walker's understanding of the history and culture of the South informs her stories of survival with a way of seeing the contemporary world and a context for expressing the accumulated meaning of life. She believes that nothing is ever "a product of the immediate present." As a result, she uses Southern history—past and recent—in order to achieve a wholeness in her fictional creations, a wholeness which she finds elusive in the private and public lives of black people. (352)

While Hurston was interested in promoting all aspects of black culture, Walker admitted that she was "preoccupied with the spiritual survival, the survival *whole* of my people," but that her specific preoccupations lay with "exploring the oppressions, the insanities, the loyalties, and the triumphs of black women. . . . For me, black women are the most fascinating creations in the world. Next to them, I place the old people—male and female—who persist in their beauty in spite of everything" (O'Brien 192). Years later, in an interview in *Black Women Writers at Work*, Walker said:

> I think my whole program as a writer is to deal with history just so I know where I am. . . . I can't move through time in any other way, since I have strong feelings about history and the need to bring it along. One of the scary things is how much of the past, especially our past, gets forgotten. (Tate 185)

While Hurston presents a people who are primarily self-sufficient, insulated from the realities of the world around them, Walker steps inside of that world to explore how the people, primarily women, are affected by all those around them, but particularly by other family members, those within the group who often visit unforgivable "sins" upon one another, usually because they have allowed the outside world, peopled and powered by whites, to render them impotent or, what is worse, unthinking and unfeeling.

Zora was to hold fast to her theme through three novels—*Jonah's Gourd Vine* (1934), *Their Eyes Were Watching God* (1937), and *Moses, Man of the Mountain* (1938)—two books of folklore—*Mules and Men* (1935) and *Tell My Horse* (1939)—an autobiography, *Dust Tracks on a Road* (1942), and a host of short stories and essays. A fourth novel, *Seraph on the Suwanee* (1948), explored a similar theme among whites. Alice Walker was to take this theme and expand it, from the inside out, describing and dissecting the woes that beset and "diminished" an individual, a couple, a family, helping them, if they would, to work through their difficulties to survive whole, ultimately and painfully to achieve that sense of "racial health" and well-being that characterized most of Hurston's fiction.

Walker's books of poetry—*Once* (1968), *Revolutionary Petunias and Other Poems* (1973), *Horses Make a Landscape More Beautiful* (1984), and *Her Blue Body* (1991); her short stories, such as "In Love and Trouble" (1973), "Good Night Willie Lee, I'll See You in the Morning" (1979), and "You Can't Keep a Good Woman Down" (1982); her novels—*The Third Life of Grange Copeland* (1970), *Meridian* (1976), *The Color Purple* (1982), *The Temple of My Familiar* (1988), and *Possessing the Secret of Joy* (1992)—and numerous essays all worry this theme. Walker tries to propel black folks first to know their past—whether the past of the civil rights movement, of twentieth-century Africa, or the millennia of *The Temple*—and second to reclaim, take control of it, and, where need be, right it, without blaming anyone for black people's missteps and misdeeds against one another, except, of course, black people themselves. In two other books, *In Search of Our Mothers' Gardens* (1983) and *Living By the Word* (1988), Walker, in an autobiographical, contemplative vein, holds forth on herself and her views in a fashion reminiscent of essays written by Zora (for example, "How It Feels to Be Colored Me"). A third edited volume, *I Love Myself When I Am Laughing . . . And Then Again When I Am Looking Mean and Impressive* (1979), pays homage to Zora, loving her primarily for loving herself and the culture she claimed as her own.

Hurston published her last literary work, *Seraph on the Suwanee*, in 1948—though she continued to write political pieces and to write fiction for which she could not find a publisher—when Alice Walker was only four years old. Zora could not know the immortality she was to enjoy when Walker discovered her as she was engaged in research for a paper on voodoo. While Zora had enjoyed some attention and notoriety during her heyday, her life had been mostly ups and downs, haunted by poverty, present and imminent, trying to balance what she wished to do—tell stories—against what others—white patron Charlotte Osgood Mason, "New Negro" black writers—demanded of her. She was devastated by many things in her life, starting with the death of her mother and continuing through the highly publicized 1948 morals charge, which sent her into a reclusive tailspin. Still, when all was said and done, she assessed the options, the payoff, and came down on the side of herself. In 1941, working on the manuscript for her autobiography, she wrote:

> While I am still far below the allotted span of time, and notwithstanding, I feel that I have lived. . . . What waits for me in the future? I do not know. I cannot even imagine, and I am glad for that. But already, I have touched the four corners of the horizon, for from hard searching it seems to me that tears and laughter, love and hate, make up the sum of life. (*Dust Tracks* 348)

On January 28, 1960, Zora Hurston died penniless in Florida, in the Saint Lucie County Welfare Home, her funeral expenses paid by family and friends, her burial place an unmarked grave in the Fort Pierce segregated cemetery, the Garden of the Heavenly Rest. She was eulogized appropriately by C. E. Bolen, owner of the *Fort Pierce Chronicle*: "Zora Neale went about and didn't care too much how she looked. Or what she said. Maybe people didn't think so much of that. But Zora Neale, every time she went about had something to offer. She didn't come to you empty" (Hemenway 348). A picaro, Zora rose and fell with the ebb and flow of life. She found her glory in the "flowing"; the trip was the thing. If she could see the light at daybreak, she did not mind the inevitable dusk. There were so many folks who had never seen the light at all.

Zora lay in the Garden of the Heavenly Rest, in whatever peace she could muster, until Alice Walker, who was fifteen when Zora died, journeyed to Fort Pierce in 1973. Walker reclaimed what she called "a Genius of the South," laying a marker on what she thought to be Zora's grave, breathing life, through her many words about Zora, back into the rich legacy that, according to Fannie Hurst (for whom Zora "worked" for a time), had "passed this way so brightly but alas, too briefly."

Thanks to Alice Walker, Hurston's biographer, Robert Hemenway, and a host of others, Zora walks brightly among us today. Her works are back in print; she is the subject of numerous books, papers, and conferences; scholarships and fellowships exist in her name; plays and television specials (most notably Ruby Dee's "Zora Is My Name") pay homage to her talents and legacy; the Zora Neale Hurston Society makes its home at Morgan State University in Baltimore, where Zora finished high school; and Eatonville, Florida, has become host to an annual Hurston conference. Indeed, the world seems to have adopted Walker's dictum: "*We are a people. A people do not throw their geniuses away.* And if they are thrown away, it is our duty as *artists and as witnesses for the future* to collect them again for the sake of our children, and, if necessary, bone by bone" (see the reprint of Walker's essay in this volume).

While almost singlehandedly resurrecting Zora, Alice Walker has achieved signal recognition in her own right, though some folks were introduced to Walker through the movie *The Color Purple*. "It is somewhat surprising," say Erma Davis Banks and Keith Byerman in their annotated bibliography of Alice Walker,

> that for many readers [Alice Walker] seemed to come suddenly on the scene with the publication of *The Color Purple*. After all, by 1982, she had been publishing poetry, fiction, and essays for fifteen years. She had by this time two novels, three books of poetry, and two collections of short stories in print, in addition to numerous stories and essays in Ms., *Black Scholar*, and other periodicals. Her work had been the subject of several scholarly articles as well as book reviews. She was one of a group of black writers, including Toni Morrison, Ernest Gaines, and Ishmael Reed, who had emerged in the late sixties and early seventies as artists whose work . . . expressed a strong sense of black heritage and pride. (xi)

Still, in 1982, Walker was virtually unknown among the masses. *The Color Purple* phenomenon—winning the Pulitzer Prize and the American Book Award, being converted to the screen by Steven Spielberg, generating lots of talk in the black community, especially among black males—firmly put the spotlight on Walker. And while *The Temple of My Familiar* has been largely ignored, public reaction to *Possessing the Secret of Joy* suggests that Walker will continue to be the center of controversial discussion.

It is Walker's enormous talent, however, the religiosity with which she insists upon telling the truth as she knows it, or as "visited onto her by the spirits," that has secured her place among the great storytellers. Like Zora, she, too, has a strong following, is the subject of conferences, television talk shows, and so forth; she, too, has scholarships awarded in her name (through the Color Purple Foundation). She, too, continues to insist upon being herself, quietly, persistently, profoundly.

To those who have read both Walker and Hurston, it is consistently and abundantly clear that, in the best tradition of what Robert Stepto, in *From Behind the Veil*, describes as the "call and response" in African-American literature, Alice Walker has responded to Zora's call, taking up her themes, varying and giving them a strident voice that resonates, unmistakenly, back to Zora.

In essays in *I Love Myself*, as well as *In Search of Our Mothers' Gardens*, and in countless interviews, Walker sketches in broad strokes the considerable ties that bind her to Zora—from discovering Zora's work on voodoo, to reading and "possessing" *Their Eyes Were Watching God*, to remembering, as she does in her 1977 essay reprinted in this volume, the first time she began to know a "Zora" existed:

> The first time I heard Zora's *name*, I was auditing a black literature class taught by the great poet Margaret Walker, at Jackson State College in Jackson, Mississippi. The reason this fact later slipped my mind was that Zora's name and accomplishments came and went so fast. . . . Jessie Fauset, Nella Larsen, Ann Petry, Paule Marshall . . . and Zora Neale Hurston were names appended, like verbal footnotes, to the illustrious all-male list that paralleled them. . . . When I read *Mules and Men* I was delighted. Here was this perfect book! . . . For what Zora's book did was this: it gave them [Walker's relatives with whom she shared the book] back all the stories they had forgotten or of which they had grown ashamed . . . and showed how marvelous, and, indeed, priceless, they are. . . . She was showing them to be: descendants of an inventive, joyous, courageous, and outrageous people; loving drama, appreciating wit, and most of all, relishing the pleasure of each other's loquacious and *bodacious* company.

In many ways, Walker's sojourn toward Zora is reminiscent of Truman Held's and Ann Marion's hankering after Meridian in Walker's novel of the same time. The seclusion Zora sought during the last decade or so of her life, Alice Walker has also sought. In many ways, Alice long ago entered the cabin in the woods vacated by Zora, became obsessively interested in her own hair, and repeated what she saw and heard. Like Meridian, Alice Walker determined long ago her real mission in life: to stand beside the road and retrieve the songs from the past we would all need to hear. Only by hearing these songs, implies Walker, can we use them to inform, temper, and help to transform our own experiences.

At this writing, Alice Walker continues to live in the woods in California, writing about people who may be geographically far away but who are certainly spiritually nearby.

2

Zora Neale Hurston: A Cautionary Tale and a Partisan View

Alice Walker

I became aware of my need of Zora Neale Hurston's work some time before I knew her work existed. In late 1970 I was writing a story that required accurate material on voodoo practices among rural Southern blacks of the thirties; there seemed none available I could trust. A number of white, racist anthropologists and folklorists of the period had, not surprisingly, disappointed and insulted me. They thought blacks inferior, peculiar, and comic, and for me this undermined, no, *destroyed*, the relevance of their books. Fortunately, it was then that I discovered *Mules and Men*, Zora's book on folklore, collecting, herself, and her small, all-black community of Eatonville, Florida. Because she immersed herself in her own culture even as she recorded its "big old lies," i.e., folk tales, it was possible to see how she and it (even after she had attended Barnard College and become a respected writer and apprentice anthropologist) fit together. The authenticity of her material was verified by her familiarity with its context, and I was soothed by her assurance that she was exposing not simply an adequate culture but a superior one. That black people can be on occasion peculiar and comic was knowledge she enjoyed. That they could be racially or culturally inferior to whites never seems to have crossed her mind.

The first time I heard Zora's *name*, I was auditing a black literature class taught by the great poet Margaret Walker, at Jackson State College in Jackson, Mississippi. The reason this fact later slipped my mind was that

Zora's name and accomplishments came and went so fast. The class was studying the usual "giants" of black literature: Chesnutt, Toomer, Hughes, Wright, Ellison, and Baldwin, with the hope of reaching LeRoi Jones very soon. Jessie Fauset, Nella Larsen, Ann Petry, Paule Marshall (unequaled in intelligence, vision, craft by anyone of her generation, to put her contributions to our literature modestly), and Zora Neale Hurston were names appended, like verbal footnotes, to the illustrious all-male list that paralleled them. As far as I recall none of their work was studied in the course. Much of it was out of print, in any case, and remains so. (Perhaps Gwendolyn Brooks and Margaret Walker herself were exceptions to this list; both poets of such obvious necessity it would be impossible to overlook them. And their work—owing to the political and cultural nationalism of the sixties—was everywhere available.)

When I read *Mules and Men* I was delighted. Here was this perfect book! The "perfection" of which I immediately tested on my relatives, who are such typical black Americans they are useful for every sort of political, cultural, or economic survey. Very regular people from the South, rapidly forgetting their Southern cultural inheritance in the suburbs and ghettos of Boston and New York, they sat around reading the book themselves, listening to me read the book, listening to each other read the book, and a kind of paradise was regained. For what Zora's book did was this: it gave them back all the stories they had forgotten or of which they had grown ashamed (told to us years ago by our parents and grandparents—not one of whom could *not* tell a story to make you weep, or laugh) and showed how marvelous, and, indeed, priceless, they are. This is not exaggerated. No matter how they read the stories Zora had collected, no matter how much distance they tried to maintain between themselves, as new sophisticates, and the lives their parents and grandparents lived, no matter how they tried to remain cool toward all Zora revealed, in the end they could not hold back the smiles, the laughter, the joy over who she was showing them to be: descendants of an inventive, joyous, courageous, and outrageous people; loving drama, appreciating wit, and, most of all, relishing the pleasure of each other's loquacious and *bodacious* company.

This was my first indication of the quality I feel is most characteristic of Zora's work: racial health; a sense of black people as complete, complex, *undiminished* human beings, a sense that is lacking in so much black writing and literature. (In my opinion, only Du Bois showed an equally consistent delight in the beauty and spirit of black people, which is interesting when one considers that the angle of his vision was completely the opposite of Zora's.) Zora's pride in black people was so pronounced in the ersatz black twenties that it made other blacks suspicious and perhaps uncomfortable (after all, *they* were still infatuated with things European). Zora was interested in Africa, Haiti, Jamaica, and—for a little racial diversity (Indians)—Honduras. She also had a confidence in herself as an individual that few people (anyone?), black or white, understood. This was because Zora grew up in a community of black people who had enormous respect for themselves and for their ability to govern themselves. Her own father had written the Eatonville town laws. This community affirmed her right to exist, and loved her as an extension of its self. For how many other black Americans is this true? It certainly isn't true for any that I know. In her easy self-acceptance, Zora was more like an uncolonized African than she was like her contemporary American blacks, most of whom believed, at least during their formative years, that their blackness was something wrong with them.

On the contrary, Zora's early work shows she grew up pitying whites because the ones she saw lacked "light" and soul. It is impossible to imagine Zora envying anyone (except tongue in cheek), and least of all a white person for being white. Which is, after all, if one is black, a clear and present calamity of the mind.

Condemned to a desert island for life, with an allotment of ten books to see me through, I would choose, unhesitatingly, two of Zora's: *Mules and Men*, because I would need to be able to pass on to younger generations the life of American blacks as legend and myth; and *Their Eyes Were Watching God*, because I would want to enjoy myself while identifying with the black heroine, Janie Crawford, as she acted out many roles in a variety of settings, and functioned (with spectacular results!) in romantic and sensual love. *There is no book more important to me than this one* (including Toomer's *Cane*, which comes close, but from what I recognize is a more perilous direction).

Having committed myself to Zora's work, loving it, in fact, I became curious to see what others had written about her. This was, for the young, impressionable, barely begun writer I was, a mistake. After reading the misleading, deliberately belittling, inaccurate, and generally irresponsible attacks on her work and her life by almost everyone, I became for a time paralyzed with confusion and fear. For if a woman who had given so much of obvious value to all of us (and at such risks: to health, reputation, sanity) could be so casually pilloried and consigned to a sneering oblivion, what chance would someone else—for example, myself—have? I was aware that I had much less gumption than Zora.

For a long time I sat looking at this fear, and at what caused it. Zora was a woman who wrote and spoke her mind—as far as one could tell, practically always. People who knew her and were unaccustomed to this characteristic in a woman, who was, moreover, a. sometimes in error, and b. successful, for the most part, in her work, attacked her as meanly as they could. Would I also be attacked if I wrote and spoke my mind? And if I dared open my mouth to speak, must I always be "correct"? And by whose standards? Only those who have read the critics' opinions of Zora and her work will comprehend the power of these questions to riddle a young writer with self-doubt.

Eventually, however, I discovered that I repudiate and despise the kind of criticism that intimidates rather than instructs the young; and I dislike fear, especially in myself. I did then what fear rarely fails to force me to do: I fought back. I began to fight for Zora and her work; for what I knew was good and must not be lost to us.

Robert Hemenway was the first critic I read who seemed indignant that Zora's life ended in poverty and obscurity; that her last days were spent in a welfare home and her burial paid for by "subscription." Though Zora herself, as he is careful to point out in his book *Zora Neale Hurston: A Literary Biography*, remained gallant and unbowed until the end. It was Hemenway's efforts to define Zora's legacy and his exploration of her life that led me, in 1973, to an overgrown Fort Pierce, Florida graveyard in an attempt to locate and mark Zora's grave. Although by that time I considered her a native American genius, there was nothing grand or historic in my mind. It was, rather, a duty I accepted as naturally mine—as a black person, a woman, and a writer—because Zora was dead and I, for the time being, was alive.

Zora was funny, irreverent (she was the first to call the Harlem Renaissance literati the "niggerati"), good-looking, sexy, and once sold hot dogs in a Washington park just to record accurately how the black people who bought the hot dogs talked. (A letter I received a month ago from one of her old friends in D.C. brought this news.) She would go anywhere she had to go: Harlem, Jamaica, Haiti, Bermuda, to find out anything she simply had to know. She loved to give parties. Loved to dance. Would wrap her head in scarves as black women in Africa, Haiti, and everywhere else have done for centuries. On the other hand, she loved to wear hats, tilted over one eye, and pants and boots. (I have a photograph of her in pants, boots, and broadbrim that was given to me by her brother, Everette. She has her foot up on the running board of a car—presumably hers, and bright red—and looks racy.) She would light up a fag—which wasn't done by ladies then (and, thank our saints, as a young woman she was never a lady) on the street.

Her critics disliked even the "rags" on her head. (They seemed curiously incapable of telling the difference between an African-American queen and

Aunt Jemima.) They disliked her apparent sensuality: the way she tended to marry or not marry men, but enjoyed them anyway—while never missing a beat in her work. They hinted slyly that Zora was gay, or at least bisexual—how else could they account for her drive? Though there is not, perhaps unfortunately, a shred of evidence that this was true. The accusation becomes humorous—and of course at all times irrelevant—when one considers that what she *did* write was one of the sexiest, most "healthily" rendered heterosexual love stories in our literature. In addition, she talked too much, got things from white folks (Guggenheims, Rosenwalds, and footstools) much too easily, was slovenly in her dress, and appeared maddeningly indifferent to other people's opinions of her. With her easy laughter and her Southern drawl, her belief in doing "cullud" dancing authentically, Zora seemed—among these genteel "New Negroes" of the Harlem Renaissance—*black*. No wonder her presence was always a shock. Though almost everyone agreed she was a delight, not everyone agreed such audacious black delight was permissible, or indeed, quite the proper image for the race.

Zora was before her time, in intellectual circles, in the life style she chose. By the sixties everyone understood that black women could wear beautiful cloths on their beautiful heads and care about the authenticity of things "cullud" *and* African. By the sixties it was no longer a crime to receive financial assistance—in the form of grants and fellowships—for one's work. (Interestingly, those writers who complained that Zora "got money from white folks" were often themselves totally supported, down to the food they ate—or, in Langston Hughes's case, *tried* to eat, after his white "Godmother" discarded him—by white patrons.) By the sixties, nobody cared that marriage didn't last forever. No one expected it to. And I do believe that now, in the seventies, we do not expect (though we may wish and pray) every black person who speaks *always* to speak *correctly* (since this is impossible): and if we *do* expect it, we deserve all the silent leadership we are likely to get.

During the early and middle years of her career Zora was a cultural revolutionary simply because she was always herself. Her work, so vigorous among the rather pallid productions of many of her contemporaries, comes from the essence of black folk life. During her later life she became frightened of the life she had always dared bravely before. Her work too became reactionary, static, shockingly misguided and timid. (This is especially true of her last novel, *Seraph on the Suwanee*, which is not even about black people, which is no crime, but is about white people for whom it is impossible to care, which is.)

A series of misfortunes battered Zora's spirit and her health. And she was broke.

Being broke made all the difference.

Without money of one's own in a capitalist society, there is no such thing as independence. This is one of the clearest lessons of Zora's life, and why I consider the telling of her life "a cautionary tale." We must learn from it what we can.

Without money, an illness, even a simple one, can undermine the will. Without money, getting into a hospital is problematic and getting out without money to pay for the treatment is nearly impossible. Without money, one becomes dependent on other people, who are likely to be—even in their kindness—erratic in their support and despotic in their expectations of return. Zora was forced to rely, like Tennessee Williams's Blanche, "on the kindness of strangers." Can anything be more dangerous, if the strangers are forever in control? Zora, who worked so hard, was never able to make a living from her work.

She did not complain about not having money. She was not the type. (Several months ago I received a long letter from one of Zora's nieces, a bright ten-year-old, who explained to me that her aunt was so proud that the only way the family could guess she was ill or without funds was by realizing they had no idea where she was. Therefore, none of the family attended either Zora's sickbed or her funeral.) Those of us who have had "grants and fellowships from 'white folks' " know this aid is extended in precisely the way welfare is extended in Mississippi. One is asked, *curtly*, more often than not: How much do you need *just to survive*? Then one is—if fortunate—given a third of that. What is amazing is that Zora, who became an orphan at nine, a runaway at fourteen, a maid and manicurist (because of necessity and not from love of the work) before she was twenty—with one dress—managed to become Zora Neale Hurston, author and anthropologist, at all.

For me, the most unfortunate thing Zora ever wrote is her autobiography. After the first several chapters, it rings false. One begins to hear the voice of someone whose life required the assistance of too many transitory "friends." A taoist proverb states that to *act sincerely with the insincere is dangerous*. (A mistake blacks as a group have tended to make in America.) And so we have Zora sincerely offering gratitude and kind words to people one knows she could not have respected. But this unctuousness, so out of character for Zora, is also a result of dependency, a sign of her powerlessness, her inability to pay back her debts with anything but words. They must have been bitter ones for her. In her dependency, it should be remembered, Zora was not alone—because it is quite true that America does not support or honor us as human beings, let alone as blacks, women, and artists. We have taken help where it was offered because we are committed to what we do and to the survival of our work. Zora was committed to the survival of her people's cultural heritage as well.

In my mind, Zora Neale Hurston, Billie Holiday, and Bessie Smith form a sort of unholy trinity. Zora *belongs* in the tradition of black women singers, rather than among "the literati," at least to me. There were the extreme highs and lows of her life, her undaunted pursuit of adventure, passionate emotional and sexual experience, and her love of freedom. Like Billie and Bessie she followed her own road, believed in her own gods, pursued her own dreams, and refused to separate herself from "common" people. It would have been nice if the three of them had had one another to turn to, in times of need. I close my eyes and imagine them: Bessie would be in charge of all the money; Zora would keep Billie's masochistic tendencies in check and prevent her from singing embarrassing anything-for-a-man songs, thereby preventing Billie's heroin addiction. In return, Billie could be, along with Bessie, the family that Zora felt she never had.

We are a people. A people do not throw their geniuses away. And if they are thrown away, it is our duty *as artists and as witnesses for the future* to collect them again for the sake of our children, and, if necessary, bone by bone.

3

Settling the Dust: Tracking Zora Through Alice Walker's "The Revenge of Hannah Kemhuff"

Mary L. Navarro and Mary H. Sims

Rarely are writers as conscious of the sources of their inspiration as Alice Walker seems to be of her connections to Zora Neale Hurston—connections that compelled her in "The Revenge of Hannah Kemhuff" to link up the experiences Zora recorded in the twenties with Walker's own mother's experiences during the Depression and to make out of them a joyous ancestral chain of continuity.[1] Rarely do authors document as thoroughly the genesis of a work as Alice Walker does her short story "The Revenge of Hannah Kemhuff," for in this story Walker brings together her two literary foremothers while at the same time fictionalizing the initial bond she formed with Zora Neale Hurston. The Hurston-Walker literary bond is deftly achieved in the narrative voice, the structure of the story, and the relationship between Tante Rosie, the rootworker, and the narrator-apprentice.

The plot of "Hannah Kemhuff" is straightforward. An elderly black woman seeks the services of the local rootworker,[2] Tante Rosie. After telling Tante and the apprentice about her malicious humiliation during the Depression at the hands of an arrogant white woman named Sarah Holley, Hannah requests that Tante place a hex on her nemesis. Tante's apprentice assists in rendering the desired outcome; the white woman dies, and Hannah is avenged. The simplicity of the action belies Walker's complex interweaving of her inspirational sources to achieve her purpose—namely to create a story that would capture both the depth of her mother's humiliation and the white woman's careless obliviousness to it. Walker uses personal experience to express a broader historical truth about the pervasive effect of white oppression and black resilience.

Black resilience is what Walker discovered in the irrepressible Zora Neale Hurston when Walker went searching for information about voodoo as it was practiced by nineteenth-century southern blacks. Not only had Walker found, through Hurston, the most definitive work on voodoo, she had also found a role model who would serve well for Walker for years to come.

Hurston's life and work have profoundly influenced Walker, and Walker pays homage to Hurston by creating Tante Rosie, whose tutelage of a novice-apprentice parallels the relationship Walker developed with her literary mentor.

Walker's mother's influence on the story is not difficult to trace, and her experience was not atypical of the humiliation and degradation blacks in America have always encountered. According to Walker, her mother went to a Red Cross center to receive flour being distributed to the needy. Her mother, who had received a box of used clothing from a sister in the north, dressed herself and three of her six children in these clothes when she went to turn in the required voucher. Noting the family's "good" clothes, one of the white women workers disdainfully turned Walker's mother away, wondering aloud about their gall for wearing better clothes than she herself had. This searing humiliation left an indelible mark on Walker's mother, who never tired of retelling the story.

Walker expands and extends her mother's experience in "Hannah Kemhuff," because her aim is to show how pervasive and far-reaching the effects of racism are. During the Depression, Hannah, much the same as Walker's mother, is rebuffed for wearing good hand-me-downs. Unlike Walker's mother, who raised eight healthy children and put three through college, Hannah's devastation is total (*In Search* 16). Denied an allotment of fatback, meal, and red beans, Hannah loses her children to starvation, one after the other. Her husband deserts her for another woman, so Hannah turns to drinking and prostitution. Stripped of all pride, love, and hope, she sinks into grief and despair; she wants to die.

When Hannah visits Tante Rosie, neither her body nor her spirit has recovered from the emotional and psychological abuse she experienced, not only from the white woman's insult that denied her and her children food to eat, but also from her husband's subsequent desertion. Hannah feels that she must act to regain her strength and a sense of purpose. Hurston's voodoo gives Walker the tool Hannah needs.

Unlike her mother, who attributed her retribution to a Christian God, Walker chooses to trust the historical and psychological beliefs of her ancestors and uses voodoo to restore Hannah's spirit. Walker's decision to use voodoo led to her discovery of Zora Neale Hurston's *Mules and Men*, where she found "the historical underpinning" she had been seeking for her story. This book gave her the frame for the mentor-protege relationship between Tante Rosie and the first-person narrator, a relationship that corresponds to Walker's initial bonding with Hurston. Hurston, in order accurately to record the history of her people, apprenticed herself to conjurers; Alice Walker in researching voodoo apprenticed herself to Zora Neale Hurston. Walker borrows liberally from *Mules and Men*, adapting Hurston's apprenticeships with various conjure doctors to her story.

The rituals and talismans Walker selects and reassembles in her story come from Part II of Hurston's *Mules and Men*, which records Hurston's study of voodoo and her apprenticeships under several two-heads (conjurers). The curse-prayer that Hannah and the apprentice intone is taken verbatim from Hurston's collection, and it is the only chant Hurston records.[3] The other voodoo elements in "Hannah Kemhuff" are Walker's adaptations. According to Hurston, voodoo elements vary with the conjurer and the situation. "Hoodoo adapts itself like Christianity to its locale, reclaiming some of its borrowed characteristics to itself" (*Mules and Men* 229). Hurston (in *Tell My Horse*, her study of Haitian history, folk practices, and voodoo) says that "voodoo is the old, old mysticism of the world in African terms and its symbolism is no better understood than that of any other religion" (137). Voodoo uses many of the same symbols and appurtenances of Christianity; candles and altars are extensions of fire worship, and the belief in the "power of water to sanctify" is symbolized by baptism (*Mules and Men* 229).

Tante Rosie's water tank, serving as a crystal ball to prophesy, is a variation of voodoo water rituals: "the spirit must have water, and if none is provided, it will wander in search of it" (248). The vinegar-dressed black candles that the apprentice and Hannah light and pray before for nine days appear in nearly every conjuring ritual invoking harm or death to an enemy. The potion of hair, nail parings, water, feces, and piece of clothing containing the odor of the enemy mixed with a pinch of goofer dust is widely employed in voodoo.[4] By combining these physical elements, the petitioner can call upon the Spirit to damn eternally the named enemy.

The "brilliant orange robe" worn by the apprentice is Walker's representation of "the crown of power" that every conjurer wears to symbolize her priesthood with the Spirit. Hurston says that preparation is required to wear the crown; however, the material of the crown may vary because "it is the meaning not the material that counts" (*Mules and Men* 246). In Walker's story, the robe "that swished and blew about [the apprentice's] legs" is what first impresses Mrs. Holley and incites her curiosity about Tante Rosie's protege.

Hannah's dialogue with Tante Rosie follows the pattern of the petitions Hurston records in her anthropological study. A petitioner seeks out a conjurer requesting that the two-head work magic. The conjurer, showing sufficient clairvoyance about the petitioner's history, induces her to reveal the problem and then proposes a voodoo ritual to achieve the desired result. The conjurer is always paid for the spell or hex.

The first part of "Hannah Kemhuff" reads like an updated version of *Mules and Men*, particularly the incident describing Hannah's discomfort with the apprentice's presence (see *In Love and Trouble* 61). The scene parallels an incident that occurred while Hurston was apprenticing under Father Watson. Sister Murchison, the petitioner, is assured that Hurston's presence is "alright. . . . She's one of us. I brought her in with me to assist and help." Hurston records the situation succinctly: "I thought still I was in her way but she told her business just the same" (*Mules and Men* 271).

Like Father Watson, Walker's narrator speaks in an intimate, conversational voice that inspires trust. Readers are immersed into Hannah Kemhuff's experience and later into the narrator's action. We trust this narrator, who, like Hurston, maintains suspense and mystery about how a curse will be effected. The narrator persuades us, just as she persuades Sarah Holley, that conjuring works.

The narrator demonstrates curiosity mixed with disbelief, arousing the same qualities in the audience. Early in the story, she admits surprise at Tante Rosie's clairvoyance, and then in a parenthetical aside tells readers that Tante (as Hurston did during her research) kept records on practically everyone.

When she tells us about the crystal ball tank of water, the narrator admits never seeing anything in there herself, though apparently Tante Rosie could (60). The narrator's approach to conjuring begins in skepticism, which the audience shares. With this note of skepticism, Walker establishes fictionally the same public attitude toward conjuring that opens Hurston's section, "Origins of Hoodoo." Hurston states that voodoo has "thousands of secret adherents. . . . [They] conceal their faith. . . . Mouths don't empty themselves unless ears are sympathetic and knowing" (*Mules and Men* 229, 231). Walker's narrator's ears are sympathetic and knowing, and the audience develops similar reactions as we listen to Hannah's degradation.

Walker begins Hannah's story, which readers learn, along with the narrator-apprentice, as eavesdroppers. The narrator-apprentice's behavior and attitude set the reader's. The compassion and intelligence of Walker's articulate narrator also engender our trust. Indeed the narrator-apprentice shows us (as does Walker's self-proclaimed commitment to Hurston) that while she is educated, she also values what Tante Rosie and Hannah represent. By using a first-person narrator who functions as a spiritual daughter to Tante Rosie, much the same as Walker does to Hurston, Walker places herself in the story and seals the bond with her newfound mentor.

The structure of "Hannah Kemhuff" also supports the Walker-Hurston bond. The story, divided into four parts, is arranged according to the narrator's increasing knowledge and her acquisition of control over the oppressor. Part I introduces the major characters in the story, Hannah's humiliation and grief, and the conjure to be performed, and concludes with Tante Rosie instructing the narrator-apprentice to assist Hannah. Part II focuses on the curse ritual, with Hannah and the apprentice reading the curse-prayer directly from *Mules and Men*. The first half of the story completes the narrator's apprenticeship and commits the narrator to Hannah's cause—revenging her spirit and removing "the burden of shame."

Parts III and IV complete the revenge and fulfill Tante's promise to Hannah: that they (Tante and her apprentice) will collect the ingredients from the patron and "dispose" of them so as to achieve maximum results—ridding the earth of Mrs. Holley before the year is over. The means to this end are cleverly achieved by the narrator-apprentice acting on minimal instruction from her mentor. Like Zora, in her apprenticeships, the narrator has earned the power and the Spirit will lead her to know what to say and do when she confronts the enemy. She is educationally and psychically prepared to bring down the oppressor without the oppressor's realizing it. Significantly, her power is words—words the tools of fiction, prose, history, folklore, and rootworking. As Byerman states, " 'The Revenge of Hannah Kemhuff' gives primacy to the mental rather than the physical power of folk practices" (140).

The spiritual bond between Tante Rosie and the narrator-apprentice mirrors the bond Walker begins with Hurston when she creates the story. Like Walker, who had only recently discovered Hurston's work, the narrator's relationship with Tante Rosie is recent. Walker's use of the affectionate appellation "Tante" is perhaps an early reference to Hurston; Walker claimed, during her pilgrimage in 1973 to Hurston's birthplace, Eatonville, Florida, that she was Hurston's niece. The French pronunciation "Ro'zee" suggests the narrator's mentor is from New Orleans which, according to Hurston, is the center of voodoo in America. Furthermore, it is the locale of Hurston's anthropological research.

Walker creates a spiritual mother-daughter relationship between the narrator-apprentice, and Hannah Kemhuff and Tante Rosie, both older than the narrator. Hannah Kemhuff is Walker's prototype of the downtrodden southern black mother. Tante Rosie (Zora) is a spiritual mother who connects the apprentice (Alice) to her history and her culture. The conjurer invests her power and wisdom in the apprentice, who will avenge all blacks by passing on the traditions, teaching pride in the race.

The narrator-apprentice is the central character through whom Alice Walker speaks. The central character is not Hannah, who, as Byerman states, "does not feel the necessity of witnessing justice; she only wants the assurance that it will happen" (140). Tante Rosie, whose instruction and knowledge supply the narrator-apprentice with the means to justice, is not the central character. The central character is the narrator-apprentice, who, by acting on Hannah's behalf to right a wrong, restores some of what had been taken from Hannah and by extension all black people as well. The neophyte conjurer must prove herself equal to the task, must prove her sincerity and her acceptance of the wisdom found in black folk beliefs, in the sympathetic magic of voodoo.

Magic is an ancient system for controlling, and conjure magic has "historically provided an access to power for a powerless people" (Hemenway 119). Hannah Kemhuff, angry at the injustice of a system that keeps her powerless, ultimately gains power over her oppressor through conjure. Whether it is the magic of the rituals Hannah performs with the apprentice or whether it is the apprentice's understanding of psychological suggestion that fulfills Hannah's revenge, the conjuring works. Hemenway states that "hoodoo (conjure) is sympathetic magic used to alter psychic and physical conditions" (120). Walker uses sympathetic magic, skillfully framing authentic voodoo rituals within a contemporary setting, and provides a plausible, rational mechanism (the power of psychological suggestion) to carry out Hannah's silent victory.

Once the apprentice completes the nine-day ritual and recitation of the curse-prayer, she assumes the mantle of power from her mentor-teacher. Tante Rosie has merely pointed the way because, as Hurston recorded, "it is not to be taught" (*Mules and Men* 250).

It is up to Tante's protege to devise a plan, to discover the means for applying Tante's instruction. By playing a mind game similar to those found in many black folktales, the narrator-apprentice gets the items Mrs. Kemhuff needs to invoke her curse from Mrs. Holley, who collects all her hair, feces, and water in plastic bags until her death, even though she assures the apprentice that she does not believe in "nigger magic." Byerman claims that "not the curse but the effort to make the curse impossible destroys Sarah Holley. Again, she seeks to deny Hannah her needs, but the denial in a perfect balancing of history becomes the vehicle of satisfaction" (141–142). Tante Rosie has taught her protege the power of words, the power of words to record history and to effect change—the same qualities Walker, in *In Search* (13), attributes to Hurston.

Whereas in Part I of "Hannah Kemhuff" the narrator plunges into the story without background or setting, Part III opens with the narrator carefully setting dates that correspond with Walker's mother's experience. Sarah Holley, born in 1910, married in 1932, the year after she had cursed and humiliated Hannah, is fifty-three in the spring of 1963 when the narrator-apprentice visits her plantation. The insult to Hannah has taken place in 1931 during the height of the Depression.

These dates correlate with Minnie Lou Walker's life. At seventeen in the late 1920s, she ran away to marry. By the time she was twenty, she had three children. Though Walker fictionalizes her mother's experience, she sets the time precisely in order to show that a curse stands until justice is done. According to her own story (*In Search* 84), the time of the story also corresponds with Walker's own beginning as a creative artist and the first time she heard of Hurston, while auditing a class in black literature. In the spring of 1963, Walker was still a student at Spelman College and just emerging as a revolutionary artist. In a talk delivered in 1970 before students at her alma mater, Sarah Lawrence, Walker called herself a black revolutionary artist and set her responsibility as creating and preserving what was created before her (*In Search* 135). For when she writes about others, she would later discover, she is really writing about herself.

Walker creates "Hannah Kemhuff" in order to preserve Hurston, her spiritual and literary foremother. Walker calls Hurston a "genius of the South" and ends her essay "A Cautionary Tale" with: "a people do not throw their geniuses away." [See essay reprinted in Chapter 2 of this volume.] Walker's secondary purpose in writing "Hannah Kemhuff" is to collect Hurston's work and make it known. This is one reason she repeats the curse-prayer, mentioning Hurston's name and work in the text. In an essay, published in 1982, Walker reprints that curse-prayer, which was already old when Hurston recorded it, and which Walker claims must have been prayed first by a colored woman (*In Search* 340). The curse-prayer, powerful in its invective and emotional in its litany of vengeance, fires the wrath and sparks the embers of hatred quite satisfyingly. The incantation moves Hannah and inspires Walker to make use of "a little hatred keenly directed" in later writings.

Part III, the confrontation of the narrator-apprentice with Mrs. Holley, demonstrates "a little hatred keenly directed." The conjurer-apprentice, on the instruction of Tante Rosie, catches the attention of the enemy by wearing a brilliant orange robe. Like Zora Neale Hurston, who knew how to dress to make a statement, the exotic garb of the apprentice arouses Mrs. Holley's curiosity and fear. Like a good lawyer, the narrator-apprentice confronts the guilty and allows her to condemn herself. In this case, the guilty is oblivious to her crime; she has the weight of history and social approval on her side. As Byerman states:

> No matter how strong their ideology or how effective their oppression, [the oppressors] cannot erase the reality of human experience, because, as Sarah Holley's obsession with her body demonstrates, they are themselves part of that reality. Despite their efforts, traces always remain of suffering and joy; giving voice to those traces delegitimizes whatever claims the system may have to truth. Those who remember and who find the strength to speak save themselves and damn the oppressors. (142)

Walker remembers her mother and her literary role model in creating "The Revenge of Hannah Kemhuff." As the narrator-apprentice, Alice Walker, spiritually and psychically bonded to these fictional counterparts, finds the strength to speak through them, thereby saving their lives and her own.

After completing her "apprenticeship," Walker assumed the mantle of power from Zora Neale Hurston, and has felt it her duty to pass it on to her people in practically everything she has written; she has celebrated Hurston's literary contributions in essays, has edited a reader composed of Zora's best pieces, and has created characters who embody this loquacious black writer. For example, in *The Color Purple*, when Celie describes a picture of Shug Avery smiling with one foot up on a car, she is describing the photograph of Hurston that appears in Robert Hemenway's Hurston biography. Shug Avery, the fun-loving womanist of *The Color Purple*, is also Zora. By creating Shug, Walker has preserved what she finds most characteristic of Zora's work: a love for self and others of the same ilk, as they are—"complete, complex, and undiminished" (*In Search* 85), and she has sealed a bond that initially began with "The Revenge of Hannah Kemhuff."

NOTES

1. "Saving the Life That Is Your Own: The Importance of Models in the Artist's Life" and "The Black Writer and the Southern Experience," both anthologized in *In Search of Our Mothers' Gardens*, document Minnie Lou Walker's experience and Zora Neale Hurston's influence on Walker's writing "The Revenge of Hannah Kemhuff." In "The

Unglamorous But Worthwhile Duties of the Black Revolutionary Artist, or the Black Writer Who Simply Works and Writes," Walker indicates how and when she learned about Hurston.

2. Hemenway states that "although many hoodoo people are also 'root doctors,' some root workers have nothing to do with hoodoo. . . . Rootwork in its strictest interpretation is fundamentally different from hoodoo and conjuring although they are often intermingled" (119).

3. The curse-prayer was given to Zora Neale Hurston by Luke Turner, who claims it was used by his aunt, Marie Leveau, the Great Voodoo Queen. Hurston became an apprentice to Turner. He was her most authentic source concerning the practices of this great conjure woman. The ritual that Turner reports that Marie Leveau performed just prior to reciting the curse-prayer closely resembles the ritual performed by Hannah and the narrator-apprentice.

4. The only reference to graveyard dust in "Hannah Kemhuff" appears on page 69 of *In Love and Trouble*. The spelling in the text is "goober" not "goofer" as Hurston records it in *Mules and Men* and in *Tell My Horse*.

WORKS CITED

Byerman, Keith E. *Fingering the Jagged Grain: Tradition and Form in Recent Black Fiction*. Athens: University of Georgia Press, 1985.

Christian, Barbara. *Black Women Novelists: The Development of a Tradition, 1892–1976*. Westport, Conn.: Greenwood Press, 1980.

Guerin, Wilfred L., et al. *A Handbook of Critical Approaches to Literature*. 2nd ed. New York: Harper and Row, 1979.

Hemenway, Robert E. *Zora Neale Hurston: A Literary Biography*. Urbana: University of Illinois Press, 1977.

Hughes, Langston, and Arna Bontemps, eds. *The Book of Negro Folklore*. New York: Dodd, Mead, 1958.

Hurston, Zora Neale. *Dust Tracks on a Road: An Autobiography*. Philadelphia: J. B. Lippincott, 1942; Urbana: University of Illinois Press, 1971, 1984.

———. *Mules and Men*. Philadelphia: J. B. Lippincott, 1935; Bloomington: Indiana University Press, 1963, 1978.

———. *Tell My Horse*. Philadelphia: J. B. Lippincott, 1938; Berkeley, Calif.: Turtle Island Press, 1981.

Walker, Alice. *The Color Purple*. New York: Harcourt Brace Jovanovich, 1982.

———. *I Love Myself When I Am Laughing . . . And Then Again When I Am Looking Mean and Impressive: A Zora Neale Hurston Reader*. New York: Feminist Press, 1979.

———. *In Love and Trouble: Stories of Black Women*. New York: Harcourt, Brace, 1973.

———. *In Search of Our Mothers' Gardens: Womanist Prose*. New York: Harcourt Brace Jovanovich, 1983.

4

Our People, Our People

Trudier Harris

Few people would doubt that Zora Neale Hurston was intimate with African-American folk culture, that she knew its forms and philosophies, the nuances of interchange between its perpetuators, and its ties to African and European cultures. Few would doubt that Hurston had an abiding respect for the culture as well as for the people. This respect occasionally manifested itself in a proprietary way, and Hurston became the gatekeeper, the medium between the folk and those who were wont to intrude upon them, much in the way that Toni Cade Bambara's Velma Henry plays that role in *The Salt Eaters* (1981). Whatever chauvinism Hurston felt, however, was ultimately forgivable because her intentions were unquestionably altruistic. She loved black people; she loved their songs and their sayings; she espoused their wisdom. She incorporated them all into her fictional works and essays about black culture.

Few people would doubt that Alice Walker is familiar with African-American folklore culture, that she has found it inspirational in the creation of her fiction, that she has a background comparable to Hurston's in touching the soil in which her people grew. She, like Hurston, knows the language of the folk, knows the forms in which they communicate with each other, knows many of the nuances of their interchanges with each other. Walker, however, is not as consistent in her attitude toward or her use of folk materials as was Hurston. Over a period of two decades, Walker's fictional depictions of African-American folk and folk forms have ranged from reverence to perversion to quiet recognition of their power.

Whereas Hurston was baptized, totally immersed in the culture from the beginning, Walker received a sprinkling. How the two authors use folk materials in their works, therefore, is the difference between intimate knowledge of the culture as usually possessed by the insider, and acquaintance with the culture as usually possessed by those who are to some extent outside. Hurston was happily in the sweetshop of African-American folk culture and could revel in that fact through years of portrayal in her works; Walker seems to have been in it in the beginning, then she went outside and pressed her nose against the sweetshop window and has had, through years of growth, to find a way to enter it again, to arrive at the point Hurston seems effortlessly to have achieved early on.

Hurston consistently has one face in the treatment of African-American folklore; that face may have subtleties of expression and movement, but it is still recognizable as one face. Walker has several faces in the depiction of African-American folk materials, some of them recognizable and some of them not. An examination of some pairings of the two authors' characters and works will perhaps make these points clearer.

In their conceptions of folk characters, both Hurston and Walker create memorable personages, and in an early example of this Walker is equally successful in her conceptualization of the African-American folk spirit. Tea Cake in Hurston's *Their Eyes Were Watching God* (1937) and Mr. Sweet in Walker's "To Hell with Dying" (1973) both have their feet set on recognizable soil. Both authors create characters who attain legendary status without compromising their credibility. It is wonderfully romantic to think of Tea Cake heroically braving raging waters to rescue Janie from a maddened dog, and it is equally romantic to think of Mr. Sweet, who by all rights should be dead from alcohol or diabetes, defying the odds again and again because the love of children keeps him alive. The not readily explained way in which Tea Cake captures the hearts of his fellow workers, and the way Mr. Sweet seems to live on nothing, also fit the mold of the larger-than-life quality of legendary characters.

There is an authentic folk quality about each character in their defiance of forces that usually daunt lesser men. Tea Cake takes on legendary proportions when he recounts to Janie the tale of his fight in a card game. Having declared himself to Janie as "one uh de best gamblers God ever made" (187), it is no wonder that the other men in the game question his seemingly miraculous skill. When they choose to take up razors to prove their point, however, they are no match for the righteously gambling, righteously fighting Tea Cake. He tells Janie:

> Baby, Ah run mah other arm in mah coat-sleeve and grabbed dat nigger by his nectie befo' he could bat his eye and then Ah wuz all over 'im jus' lak gravy over rice. He lost his razor tryin' tuh git loose

> from me. He wuz hollerin' for me tuh turn him loose, but baby, Ah turnt him every way *but* loose. (190–191)

The greased lightning quality of his movements, combined with his appropriation of general folk expressions to his own actions ("turning him every way but loose"), serves to put Tea Cake firmly in the tradition of those men who fare well no matter the situations in which they find themselves.

Mr. Sweet seems miraculous not only in his ability to be nearly blind drunk and sober at the same time, but also in his ability not to seem larger than he is but smaller. By so doing, he breaks down the barriers between adults and children, thereby endearing himself to the narrator and her siblings.

Mr. Sweet and Tea Cake are both bluesmen who belong to the world; the women and children in their lives may have intangible claims on them, but they can never expect those claims to hold sway unless the bluesmen want such commitment. Mr. Sweet is perhaps what an older Tea Cake might have become—slightly mysterious in his past, generally attractive to those around him, possessing a special talent with music, defying the natural odds of life and death. There are folk counterparts to both figures in the romantic men who have no material attachments to the world, who want little more than the comfort of music and a place to lay their heads at the end of the day. Like Jimboy in Hughes's *Not Without Laughter* (1931), or Big Boy in Sterling Brown's "The Odyssey of Big Boy," *life* keeps these men alive; they belong to the air and to a tradition that they have the pleasure of representing for a short time in its long continuum. Their needs are small; their complaints are few; their vision is larger than that of those mired in the clay around them.

Both men in their early lives exhibit the carefree status popular in the mythology of the roving bluesman, the one with the guitar slung over his shoulder—like Luzana Cholly in *Train Whistle Guitar* (1974) or John Lee Hooker in "Hobo Blues"—making his way to the nearest empty freight car for another jaunt into the unknown. When Tea Cake takes Janie fishing at midnight or to the church picnic, or when he lounges as if he has not a care in the world, or when he goes gambling, the mentality of the roving bluesman holds sway, and Janie is rightfully concerned that the young man may love her and leave her, for the backdrop against which he is conceived reveres that mobility. But Janie is the good blueswoman able to make the roving man give up his traveling ways—or at least take her along with him.

A mysterious part of his early life enhances Mr. Sweet's bluesman status, as speculative details generally heighten the value of legend. Married to

Miss Mary and reputed to be the father of her shiftless son, Mr. Sweet has somehow been wronged in love. It is from his singing the blues that the narrator learns that Mr. Sweet was forced to marry Miss Mary even though he loved someone else who now lived in a different city, somewhere up north. Besides, he was not sure that Miss Mary's baby was his own.

Faithless love is one of the trademarks of the blues tradition, and scarred lovers like Mr. Sweet testify to its unfaithfulness. His story is so poignant that the narrator wishes she had been Mr. Sweet's gal, old enough to love him and have him love her back. Mr. Sweet's character works for Walker, as Tea Cake's does for Hurston, because she is able to achieve an aura of authenticity with him that readily places him in a recognizable tradition.

Even the title, "To Hell with Dying," places him in that oral tradition; it has kinship to those legendary balkers at death, including Big Sixteen (Hughes and Bontemps), Staggolee (Abrahams 129–142), and others of the "tombstone disposition, graveyard mind" mentality. Not only does Big Sixteen stare death unblinkingly in the face, but when he is finally subdued and arrives in hell, he is so cantankerous that the devil gives him a piece of fire to go off and start his own little private hell. "Death can't hinder me," so the religious/mythic legend goes, and for a time, Mr. Sweet writes his name among those who utter the phrase. The fact that the narrator calls his resurrections "revivals" (132, 134, 135) also extends the legendary/religious/mythic tie. Mr. Sweet keeps coming back to life from a deathlike state, each time defying the odds of biology. When he actually dies at the age of ninety, that is also a kind of defiance, for black men generally do not live to such a ripe old age.

Walker's characterization of Mr. Sweet is successful in part because the narrator's tone is so quiet and believable. We are predisposed to respond favorably toward him because he is such an integral part of the young girl's growing process; her innocence and belief, her wanderlust, encourage our own. Walker makes no effort to force the folk material upon us; it comes naturally as the interior lives of the characters unfold. Mr. Sweet is an integral part of the domestic landscape, not superimposed upon it, just as Tea Cake flows naturally into the fabric of the story of Janie's life. Both portrayals are successful because, when held up against the tradition of their conceptions, all the shadowed outlines coincide.

When Walker turns to the exterior landscape, however, her characterization of folk character and belief is less successful. Consider, on the one hand, Walker's "Strong Horse Tea" and "The Revenge of Hannah Kemhuff," and Hurston's "Spunk" and "Uncle Monday." In her stories, Walker diverges from a recognizable tradition and creates a rendition of the folk culture, especially in "Strong Horse Tea," that one of my colleagues refers to as a "perverse grotesque." In that story, the folk culture becomes the basis for undermining human integrity, not supporting it. Ralph Ellison, in an often quoted passage, asserts that African-American folk culture enabled black people to trust their own sense of reality, their own sense of value, against the negative opinions of those who sought to define them. "Strong Horse Tea" posits that the African-American folk culture is not only untrustworthy, but that those who hold to its beliefs are almost demented.

Certainly there is a possibility that Aunt Sarah might not be able to cure Rannie Toomer's baby by working her roots on it, but the skeptical attitude that Rannie holds leads her to disrespect not only the representative of the tradition but the tradition itself. By allowing Rannie Toomer to view Aunt Sarah as a witch or a wielder of "nigger magic," and by sending her out into the pouring rainstorm in search of horse urine, Walker humiliates the woman and disrespects the love she presumably has for her child. The harmony that exists between the legendary, romantic, or supernatural world and the real one in "To Hell with Dying" is disrupted in "Strong Horse Tea." Natural phenomena become obstacles to human endeavor and indeed create a supranatural, surrealistic setting in the story.

Even as Rannie has stood talking with the postman, encouraging him to get a "REAL doctor" for her baby, she has been made to seem out of balance with the world around her, unaware of the reality of racial politics. When she distrusts the reality of Aunt Sarah to the point that she is forced to go rushing after the retreating mare, gathering her precious cargo, and using her mouth to stop the leak in her shoe, she is again out of balance, disruptive. The disruption has its basis less in what Rannie does than in the options Walker has carved out for her. Essentially, she is in the impossible situation of being damned if she believes in the "REAL doctor" and damned if she believes in Aunt Sarah's power.

Her creation is intended to show the futility of her position as a lone female, with a child, in the middle of nowhere. Walker imposes feminist politics upon the folk culture and makes it one of the villains; it is therefore not the flexible, recognizable concept we usually think of as African-American folk in origin, but a monster used to degrade Rannie even further. The result is that readers consider Rannie's plight less than worthy of their sustained attention because Walker severely alters the tradition on her way to putting forth her thesis. In this manifestation, the face of the folk is not familiar.

In contrast, Hurston's foray into that exterior, natural realm of the folk culture in "Spunk" posits the extranatural belief as "natural" within the set of circumstances she has created. When Spunk steals the timid Kelsey's girlfriend and parades his conquest before the cowardly man, the neighbors take an active, gossipy role in speculating on what the result of such brazen behavior can be. When Spunk kills Joe Kelsey and is himself killed in a sawmill accident, they also help in creating the legendary explanation for Spunk's demise—Kelsey's ghost has pushed him into the saw. The sequence of events as set forth establishes the logic of cause and effect that is peculiar to the folk; there is a poetic justice in what the neighbors believe has happened to Joe, and it fits with their folk values of punishment being meted out to the erring.

Traditionally, one of the reasons ghosts are believed to return is to right the wrongs left unsettled before their deaths: an unattentive mother may be punished for not taking care of her children, a robber may be uncovered, or a murderer may be brought to justice. And individuals who were themselves killed are notoriously reputed to return; whenever strange occurrences take place in or near their place of death, the murdered one's restless spirit is credited with the disturbance. In "Spunk," the *community* acts as a chorus in offering the correct interpretation of the sequence of events even as it simultaneously perpetuates those events through the storytelling process. Without such a medium of exchange, or such a backdrop of support in "Strong Horse Tea," Rannie's story is effectively lifted out of context, where folk logic does not apply and cannot serve to explain what has happened to her in either realistic or legendary terms.

The community context is equally important in creating the aura of folk credibility in Hurston's "Uncle Monday," whereas in Walker's "The Revenge of Hannah Kemhuff," that factor, though hinted at, is more academic or superimposed than intrinsic. The competition between the two conjurers—Uncle Monday and Aunt Judy Bickerstaff—takes on mythic proportions that are augmented by community commentary. Uncle Monday is so different when he appears that people begin to create explanations for his unique qualities. In a setting that lends itself to wonderment, in which natural phenomena such as alligators grow to legendary size, it is not farfetched to connect Uncle Monday to the otherworldly.

People in the community, such as Lindsay, Emma Lou Pittman, and Merchant, add credence to Uncle Monday's supernatural powers with their narratives about encounters with him. Lindsay recalls that he has seen Uncle Monday actually walking on the lake, and Mrs. Pittman recounts visiting him once only to be greeted by "a great growling and snapping of mighty jaws," the sight of Uncle Monday's "horribly mangled" right arm, and a trail of blood leading to his cabin (*The Sanctified Church*

32). Merchant's testimony is hardest for the neighbors to believe, but it is in keeping with the overall circumstances surrounding Uncle Monday: Merchant relates that he saw a huge alligator come out of the lake, shapeshift itself from animal to man as it walked along a path, and appear in town as Uncle Monday.

It is not surprising for the community to believe, therefore, that Uncle Monday has proven once and for all who is the greatest conjurer by walking on water and commanding his alligator friends to accost Aunt Judy when she is out fishing; he has rooted her to the spot, made it impossible for her to move or leave her fishing site. He appears to her in a "bar of red light" and asserts that her "bragging tongue" has brought her there and will keep her there until she acknowledges in her heart that he is her "master." He then disappears and leaves a huge alligator to watch as she tries desperately to keep her head above the shallow water in which she is lying. After waiting in terror for hours to be rescued, and after losing part of the use of her legs, Aunt Judy concedes that Uncle Monday is indeed the most powerful conjurer. She in fact perpetuates his status by telling the story of what has happened to her, by becoming a functioning member of the community of active tradition bearers who retell the lore.

In "The Revenge of Hannah Kemhuff," Walker again lifts the folk beliefs out of their context—or creates an atypical context for them—by holding them up to the light of practicality and finding them wanting. She demystifies the conjuring process by explaining that Tante Rosie has cardboard files on various townspeople; the clairvoyant quality of the conjurer is thereby reduced to petty sneaking. The role of the narrator continues that demystification, for she suggests that conjuration is just another academic course to be passed, that there is no unnamable, extranatural quality to it, few, if any, of those special traits identified by Newbell Niles Puckett in *Folk Beliefs of the Southern Negro* (1926). Seeking revenge on "the little moffet" is reduced to being a matter of getting enough information to make the woman eliminate herself. The conjure woman is thus more a fashion model than a force of power of the likes of Aun' Peggy in Charles W. Chesnett's *The Conjure Woman* (1899), for Tante Rosie has no community to relate tales of her power, no victims whispering what she has done to them, no real legitimacy as a *traditional* conjurer. Mrs. Holley succeeds in scaring and starving herself to death, but Tante Rosie's and the narrator's roles in her demise are more a study in parody than in power.

The demystification of the conjuring process extends as well to the breakdown of the traditional distance between fiction and reality. As if making a direct link to those reading the book, Walker allows Mrs.

Kemhuff and the narrator to read the curse-prayer for Mrs. Holley directly from Zora Neale Hurston's *Mules and Men* (1935). Again, conjuring is presented as being something one can acquire from textbooks and interviews, not something that needs any inherent power in those executing the spells. Nor does it need any compliant community perpetuating it. Mrs. Holley's personal maid, Caroline, does comment on what is happening to her former employer, but she does so in the context of informing the narrator about the "spell," not perpetuating the lore to someone who has not had any contact with the original plans.

Clearly, Walker and Hurston have different philosophical approaches to the use of African-American folk traditions. For Hurston, the artist's imagination distills the raw material of the culture and transforms it in art into something that mirrors that culture, something that is authentic and accurate in its reflection of the culture. Walker has less of a sustained, lucid response to the culture. In some works, she exhibits a closeness to it; in others, there is a distance that would make Hurston consider her a wayward child rather than a kindred spirit.

Both authors, however, seem to hold equal appreciation for African-American folk speech. In Hurston's *Jonah's Gourd Vine* (1934), and Walker's *The Color Purple* (1982), for example, they create characters who could very easily have walked in the soils of Florida and Georgia; indeed, in this arena, Walker may not be more imaginative than Hurston, but she is at times more successful in using folk speech in context. This comparison may be mitigated somewhat by the fact that *Jonah's Gourd Vine* is Hurston's first book and *The Color Purple* is Walker's third, but the comparison is nonetheless valid.

Jonah's Gourd Vine is the one instance in which Hurston appears to be overwhelmed by a facet of folk culture, namely folk speech. She is overwhelmed in the sense that she allows her fascination for the speech to overtake her artistic sense. The language the characters use itself becomes a character in that it takes center stage instead of supporting the various emotions being conveyed. This is the one work in Hurston's canon in which the folk element seems superimposed rather than evolving naturally out of the fictional setting.

In situations in which arguments erupt between characters, the expressions of anger and the dares they use come straight from collected black folk expressions. For example, when Ned Crittenden calls his wife, Amy, a liar, her retort is: "Youse uh nother one, Ned Crittenden! Don't you lak it, don't you take it, heah mah collar come and shake it!" (17). This makes them sound like naughty children challenging each other on a playground instead of grownups who started a disagreement about the amount of work

John, Amy's illegitimate oldest son, should do in compensation for his stepfather's financial support. Later, when John's wife, Lucy, is on her deathbed, she chastises her husband for his unfaithfulness: "Go 'head on, Mister, but remember—youse born but you ain't dead. 'Tain't nobody so slick but why they kin stand uh 'nother greasin'. Ah done told yuh time and time uhgin dat ignorance is de hawse dat wisdom rides. Don't git miss-put on yo' road. God don't eat okra" (204). Perhaps these could be envisioned as the words of a woman near death, but we forget her situation as we focus on the words in and of themselves.

The result of such exchanges is that the traditional, formulaic speech presumably becomes the old mold into which new wine is poured, except that readers become so fascinated with the mold that they forget its contents. Indeed, Hurston offers one instance where readers focus exclusively on the language. After an altercation with his stepfather, in which Ned threatens to go home, get his gun, and return to shoot him, John waits behind a tree and gives it Ned's identity for his onslaught of words:

> And you, you ole battle-hammed, slew-foot, box-ankled nubbin, you! You ain't nothin' and ain't got nothin' but whut God give uh billy-goat, and then round tryin' tuh hell-hack folks! Tryin' tuh kill somebody wid talk, but if you wants tuh fight,—dat's de very corn Ah wants tuh grind. You come grab me now and Ah bet yuh Ah'll stop *you* from suckin' eggs. Hit me now! G'wan hit me! Bet Ah'll break uh egg in yuh! Youse all parts of uh pig! You done got me jus' ez hot ez July jam, and Ah ain't got no mo' use fuh yuh than Ah is for mah baby shirt. Youse mah race but you sho ain't mah taste. Jus' you break uh breath wid me, and Ahm goin' tuh be jus' too chastisin'.
>
> Ahm jus' lak uh old shoe—soft when you rain on me and cool me off, and hard when yuh shine on me and git me hot. Tuh keep from killin' uh sorry somethin' like yuh, Ahm goin' way from heah. Ahm goin' tuh Zar, and dat's on de other side of far, and when you see me agin Ahm gointer be somebody. Mah li'l' finger will be bigger than yo' waist. Don't you part yo' lips tuh me no mo' jes' ez long ez heben is happy—do Ah'll put somethin on yuh dat lye soap won't take off. You ain't nothin' but uh big ole pan of fell bread. Now dat's de word wid de bark on it. (85–86)

No matter how much we appreciate the folk creativity in the phrasing, or try to attribute the use of such metaphors to John's youthful exploration with language (as in the "man of words" tradition), we still cannot get around the fact that Hurston includes the scene primarily to satisfy her love for folk expressions, to give vent to sayings that she cannot possibly use in a carefully integrated conversation in the text. It is appropriate that the chapter ends with this harangue, for it has been the love of formulaic language that has prompted Hurston's depiction of an altercation between John and his stepfather, not the disagreement itself.

On the other hand, when Hurston uses formulas in a religious context, they are equally rooted in the tradition, but inappropriate in some instances to the characters who utter them. In a prayer that the teenage John utters, Hurston takes the formulas directly from African-American oral tradition.

> Oh, Lawd, heah 'tis once mo' and again yo' weak and humble servant is knee-bent and body-bowed—Mah heart beneath mah knees and mah knees in some lonesome valley cryin' fuh mercy whilst mercy kinst be found. O Lawd! You know mah heart, and all de ranges uh mah deceitful mind—and if you find any sin lurkin' in an about mah heart please pluck it out and cast it intuh de sea uh fuhgitfullness whar it'll never rise tuh condemn me in de judgment. (51–52; see also 138, 145)

The rhythms and phrases of John's prayer have been recorded by Hurston in other sources from her collecting days among black people, and they parallel almost exactly many of the formulas James Weldon Johnson uses in his "Listen Lord, A Prayer," the first section of *God's Trombones* (1927), the volume he created as a result of listening to black church services.

We can applaud Hurston's faithfulness to the tradition, but wonder if the young John, who has been playing hide and seek and has witnessed a couple of girls fighting over him a matter of hours earlier, is really aware of the import of the words or the spirit they are intended to capture. Such words are usually uttered by seasoned veterans in the religious experience, such as deacons and mothers of the church.

By contrast, Walker succeeds in *The Color Purple* in giving us a book saturated with folk speech; no matter our approval or disapproval of the incidents conveyed, they are conveyed in the authentic voice of the folk. Celie's voice never seems detached from or intrusive upon the situations she presents; it is smoothly integrated into the overall aura of the book. Her first-person narration may be viewed as keeping within the storytelling vein of African-American oral delivery. Walker captures the rhythms as well as the nuances of African-American speech, including signifying and subtle humor, as in the passage in which Celie comments on Harpo eating himself into a size suitable for combat with his wife Sofia.

Walker's folk speech is clearly a medium, not an obstacle; it facilitates meaning rather than competing with it. The folk quality is inherent in the narration, not clustered in conversations at intervals in the story. Consequently, the total effect is of a complete merging, a saturation, instead of a battle between the potentially opposing elements of language and events.

Arguments in Walker's novel may be fraught with the flavor of folk speech, but that speech does not detract from the disagreements themselves, which deservedly take center stage. When Celie encounters Albert as she is about to depart for Memphis with Shug, not only is she ready to play the dozens, but she is ready to back up her action by stabbing Albert in the hand when he tries to slap her for her impudence. John and Ned's encounter is all "form and fashion and outside show to the world"; neither man is ready to follow through with physical violence. Celie's is a transformation, a shapeshifting, that is achieved in spirit and manifested in words ("conversion" is another term that could be applied to her change, thus re-rooting her in the religious/folk tradition of her early years, but without the same kinds of entrapments).

The metaphors Celie uses are drawn from the natural and domestic environments to which the folk against which her character is conceived were generally exposed; such metaphors are appropriate without being ostentatious. In terms of successful use of folk speech, therefore, Walker fares as well in *The Color Purple* as Hurston does in any of her fictional creations.

Not only do these two authors use folklore in their fiction, but they themselves have become subjects of African-American folklore. Stories float about them as readily as they do about some of the characters they created. Hurston's exploits during the Harlem Renaissance, for example, have been cited by Langston Hughes in his autobiography as well as by various of her biographers. Her appearances and disappearances are the subject of much speculation, as are the details of her marriages. What happened to her after 1948 is as much the stuff of legend as it is the biography of a writer—working as a maid after initial successes, living and dying in poverty, being buried through donations. Even the fact that Alice Walker has played a key role in the revival of interest in Hurston's life and work is another facet of the legend-making process, for certainly in recent years Hurston has become larger than life. Walker is one of the active tradition bearers who keeps the legend and legacy of Zora Neale Hurston alive; her "search" for Zora Neale Hurston compares favorably with Hurston's collecting for *Mules and Men.*

Walker has joined Hurston in becoming legendary. Her phenomenal successes over the past decade have kept her alive and well in the oral tradition, for word-of-mouth responses to her work, especially to *The Color Purple*, have been as significant in perpetuating the reputation of the novel as the story itself. Her near-reclusive existence over the past few years, combined with her comments on the spiritualist method of composition for her works, lend themselves equally well to an oral tradition fired by the outlines of detail without the minute specificity that stunts imagination. Both of these women writers, therefore, have been claimed by the very folk traditions that have served as inspiration to their creative endeavors; they provide striking examples of the strength of African-American folk culture as process and as art.

WORKS CITED

Abrahams, Robert D. *Deep Down in the Jungle: Negro Narrative Folklore from the Streets of Philadelphia*. Chicago: Aldine, 1970.

Hughes, Langston, and Arna Bontemps, eds. *The Book of Negro Folklore*. New York: Dodd, Mead, 1958.

Hurston, Zora Neale. *Jonah's Gourd Vine*. Philadelphia: J. B. Lippincott, 1934, 1971.

——. *Mules and Men*. Philadelphia: J. B. Lippincott, 1935; Bloomington: Indiana University Press, 1963, 1978.

——. *The Sanctified Church*. Berkeley, Calif.: Turtle Island Press, 1981.

——. *Their Eyes Were Watching God*. Philadelphia: J. B. Lippincott, 1937; Urbana: University of Illinois Press, 1978.

Walker, Alice. *The Color Purple*. New York: Harcourt Brace Jovanovich, 1982.

——. *In Love and Trouble: Stories of Black Women*. New York: Harcourt, Brace, 1973.

II

Their Eyes Were Watching God and *The Color Purple*

5

A Sense of Wonder: The Pattern for Psychic Survival in *Their Eyes Were Watching God* and *The Color Purple*

Alice Fannin

If one sets out to explore the bonds and similarities between black women writers, the rich connections reaching back nearly half a century from Alice Walker to Zora Neale Hurston are surely inescapably intriguing. Walker, who of course never met Hurston, has nonetheless connected herself to Hurston by the admiration expressed for her in a variety of essays and forewords, and by the effort invested in producing an anthology of Hurston's work in order to retrieve it from an ungenerous past. Walker even sought out Hurston's unmarked grave and placed a marker on it—as one might an ancestor's or kinswoman's—thus in a way returning both the body of the author and her work to history and to us.

Examining their literary kinship, we discover the wellspring of their similarities: the South, with its land and seasons as a backdrop for the life described in their most important novels; and the richness of black life and traditions—the laughter, the language, and the folklore. Finally, though each author speaks out of her own time and place, we are not surprised that in the mysterious workings of the imagination, bits and pieces of life remembered and life imagined from such a common past coalesce like iron filings around a magnet, producing parallels, similar patterns.

One of the most distinctive similarities is the theme in each author's major novel, Hurston's *Their Eyes Were Watching God* and Walker's *The Color Purple*. Each novel initially pictures the black woman as the one human being in society to whom almost anything can be done—and usually is. Nanny Crawford in *Their Eyes* could be speaking for either Janie

First printed in the *Zora Neale Hurston Forum* 1.1 (1986): 1–11. Reprinted by permission.

Crawford or Celie of *Color Purple* when she describes the black woman, given her political, social, and familial circumstances, as the mule of the world: "So de white man throw down de load and tell de nigger man tuh pick it up. He pick it up because he have to, but he don't tote it. He hand it to his woman folks. De nigger woman is de mule of the world so fur as Ah can see" (29). Though this much celebrated passage could, of course, be true of many black women's lives and certainly many are described as such by other novelists, this passage does not adequately convey either Hurston's or Walker's final theme.

Both authors instead take their protagonists on a quest that is psychological and, most importantly, spiritual—and to a lesser degree, even cosmological and ontological. Obviously the quest motif is ubiquitous in literature, but the differences here are that male characters, often by both interior and exterior journeys, increase their influence or power in personal, social, or political circumstances; many female characters, their self-knowledge and independence. Janie and Celie, however, go beyond the level of all these to an exploration of self as part of the universe and the universe as part of the self.

Both women first endure a series of trials that threaten psychic extinction, death-in-life; both are moved by another person's love as a catalyst to begin to love and value themselves; yet both finally attain the self-worth necessary to survive alone. To do this, each protagonist discovers, fortunately for the sake of survival, a "sense of wonder." Each comes to recognize that she is a unique entity in the plenitude of Creation and that her place, however finite, is an integral part of a mysterious and wonder-working process that created, and is always creating and re-creating, an infinite universe. Believing this, neither Janie nor Celie will allow earthly circumstances to diminish that particular sense of self-worth. For each woman, then, psychic survival depends not so much on greater self-awareness and independence—though they gain that too—but on the vision of the self as a wondrous part of a Creation that is itself "wondrously and fearfully" made.

Though Walker carries her theme through events and the significance of the color purple to a direct and climactic statement in the next-to-last letter, Hurston suggests it indirectly through three major patterns of imagery. As *Their Eyes Were Watching God* begins, Janie Crawford is trying to explain to her closest friend Pheoby the conflict between the roles others intend for her and the potential she vaguely understands she should search for. At this point the novel introduces two distinctive patterns of imagery, the pear tree and the horizon. A now middle-aged Janie narrating the story remembers that "her conscious life had commenced at Nanny's gate" (23), that day at age sixteen when she moved from lying under a snowy pear tree in bloom to wandering through her grandmother's garden. Eve-like, she wandered the garden, "seeking confirmation of the voice and vision [emanating from the pear tree], and everywhere she found and acknowledged answers. A personal answer for all other creations except for herself" (24).

Even though young Janie can find no immediate answers, she knows that the pear tree "has called her to come and gaze on a mystery. From barren brown stems to glistening leaf-buds; from the leaf-buds to snowy virginity of bloom. It stirred her tremendously" (23). Watching "a dust-bearing bee sink into the sanctum of a bloom; the thousand sister-calyxes arch to meet the love embrace," Janie thinks: "So this was marriage!" (24).

At this point, her only perception of her place in this wondrous process is sexual, to be part of the creation of life.

> She was sixteen. She had glossy leaves and bursting buds and she wanted to struggle with life but it seemed to elude her. Where were the singing birds for her? Nothing on the place nor in her grandma's house answered her. She searched as much of the world as she could from the top of the steps and then went on down to the front gate and leaned over to gaze up and down the road. . . . Waiting for the world to be made. (25)

Eve-like and as yet still innocent, Janie has come to the consciousness of the separateness of her being, her individual selfhood, in this metaphoric garden as world. Dimly aware that all of Creation partakes of a mystery and that all things in it fulfill their appointed places (have their answers), she is not yet sure of her value in the scheme.

Janie's intuition, since she is experiencing a sexual awakening also, is that she is connected to the pear tree in terms of life-bearing fruitfulness. Hurston, educated as an anthropologist, is no doubt quite deliberate in her use of both the pear and other trees, knowing (probably from Frazer's discussions) that in primitive cultures pear trees and other fruit-bearing trees symbolize the sexuality/fertility of women, and also that trees in general symbolize simply the life force itself.

Both types of awakenings, to one's own self and to one's sexuality, are implied here. Though Janie will not bear any children, she will recognize her place in the scheme of Creation. At the present, caught in the narrow confines of Nanny's house and closed behind the gate, Janie can only look impatiently at the road that leads to the horizon, waiting for the world to be made, not knowing yet that it cannot be made for her; she must create it herself.

Though the pear tree and the road to the horizon are before her, Janie's desire to learn the answer to her existence and her options to do so are limited by her grandmother. Nanny, also delineated by the tree imagery, is described not as a living tree, but a ruined one. "Nanny's head and face looked like the standing roots of some old tree that had been torn away by storm. Foundation of ancient power that no longer mattered" (26). Nanny, a former slave, may once have been as rich with the promise of life as Janie is. Certainly there are clues that her white master, who left her pregnant with his child and went off to join the final battles of the Civil War, found her so. Perhaps the promise of life for herself and baby daughter was also symbolized in her choice of the baby's name, Leafy. And when fear for Leafy's safety gives Nanny the courage to run away from the white world, she wraps Leafy in moss and hides her temporarily in a tree. But Nanny can find no place except as a menial, and no real safety in the world.

After Leafy's rape and ruin, Nanny decides that safety lies in the propriety and property ownership so valued by white society. When she catches Janie kissing shiftless Johnny Taylor and believes Janie's sexual ruin is imminent, Nanny uses her own personal history to demonstrate to her granddaughter that the black woman is the "mule of the world," a "spit cup" for menfolks black and white. Nanny's solution is to give Janie propriety by the legalities of white society, a marriage "same as Mis Washburn's" (40), the white woman Nanny works for, and property ownership by an arranged marriage.

She forces sixteen-year-old Janie into marriage to Logan Killicks, an old widower with sixty acres, whose face, according to Janie, resembles a skull-head in the graveyard and whose person has the musty odor of death about it. With no authority to refute the power of history, age, and property represented by Nanny and Logan, Janie accepts mutely. Certainly she cannot explain that "the vision of Logan Killicks was desecrating the pear tree," which to Janie represents her blooming selfhood; nor is she aware that she foreshadows her own fate in her description of his home as a "stump in the middle of the woods" (39). There Killicks attempts to "kill" Janie's spirit, to reduce the pear tree to a stump by making her a work mule, the fate Nanny so abhorred.

Later, when Joe Starks comes by, Janie recognizes that "he did not represent sun-up and pollen and blooming trees, but he spoke for far horizon" (50). Throwing off her apron and, she hopes, her menial role, she leaves with Starks for the horizon, trying to believe he might be a "bee for her bloom" (54), but Joe soon begins to take the "bloom off of things" (70). By refusing to allow Janie to participate in community talkfests on his store porch, urging her not to associate with the "common women" in the community, and convincing her that she must maintain her seat in the "high chair" he has given her by his wealth and position, Joe imprisons Janie in "starkest" isolation. Finally, Janie realizes that her marriage is dead, that Joe wants only "her submission" (111), that she gets "nothing from Jody except what money could buy," and that she "was giving away what she didn't value" (118). She concludes: "Ah ain't got nothin' tuh live for" (118). She then makes herself unfeeling as the earth, "which soaks up urine and perfume with the same indifference" (119).

Janie has been reduced from a celebrant of a wondrous creation to a figure of death-in-life. The narrative voice informs us that she suffers this change because as yet she "didn't know that she was the world and heavens boiled down to a drop" (119). She is not just a contributing element of Creation, but contains infinity's wonder in her self. To desecrate her self is to desecrate creation. She should not, in fact must not, derive the quality of her life from Joe nor even from their marriage; though she is minuscule as a drop, she must find within herself her importance in the universe.

At this point, Janie continues to believe that she should explore external horizons. The reader is aware, however, that the horizon imagery introduced in the novel's first two paragraphs delineated an important difference between men's and women's journeys to the horizon. The narrative voice explained in the opening paragraphs that in men's lives, events predominate over all; men deal practically with that horizon out there where ships do come in or else sail by, thus shaping life and dreams. Women, however, create an inner world, shaping its horizons themselves by choosing "to forget all those things they don't want to remember" and by remembering "everything they don't want to forget. The dream is the truth. Then they act and do things accordingly" (9). For whatever reason, innate or enculturated, women's journeys, as the novel describes them, are expansive of the emotional life in an interior world.

After Joe's death, the horizon metaphor reappears as Janie reenters life and renews her search for the horizon with greater maturity and understanding. Janie knows now that internal freedom can be restricted just as much as external freedom, and recognizes that Nanny, whom she had so loved and believed, imposed a major restriction on her.

> She [Janie] had been getting ready for her great journey to the horizons in search of people; it was important to all the world that she should find them and they find her. But she had been whipped

> like a cur dog, and run off down a back road after things. It was all according to the way you see things. Some people could look at a mud-puddle and see an ocean with ships. But Nanny belonged to that other kind that loved to deal in scraps. Here Nanny had taken the biggest thing God ever made, the horizon—for no matter how far a person can go the horizon is still way beyond you—and pinched it in to such a little bit of a thing that she could tie it about her granddaughter's neck tight enough to choke her. (138)

Nanny had allowed no expansiveness of the self, no trying out the fullness of human potential. She had restricted internal horizons even more than external ones.

As Janie begins to explore her internal horizons, a third, related pattern of imagery, that of light, sun, and spark, emerges. Through it, Janie articulates her mythic version of the origin and universal importance of human beings. Though she feels she has been terribly misused, has been "set in the market place to sell" and used "for still-bait," despite her degradation, she argues that

> when God had made the man, he made him out of stuff that sung all the time and glittered all over. Then after that some angels got jealous and chopped him into millions of pieces, but still he glittered and hummed. So they beat him down to nothing but sparks but each little spark had a shine and a song. So they covered each one over with mud. And the lonesomeness in the sparks make them hunt for one another, but the mud is deaf and dumb. (138–139)

Janie's myth of human origins is not exactly orthodox, and thus should not be interpreted in a closely orthodox Christian system, for neither Hurston in real life nor Janie in the novel is orthodox. Not abiding by the conventional Christian tenets that offer salvation and resurrection, Janie assumes only that the spark of humanity (not divinity) is each person's individual being and that the particular function of humankind is simply to be, to develop one's humanity as expansively as possible. As the pear tree has its answer, this is the answer for humanity.

In the conjunction of the two imagistic patterns above, the journey to the horizon (not in actual distance a journey at all) is the necessary expansion of the spirit to its fullest potential. A person must not, cannot, be limited to dealing only with things, with scraps; interaction with other human beings who have in them that same spark allows for the full exercise of humanity and humaneness, an exercise necessary for spiritual growth.

Fortunately, Tea Cake Woods appears in the novel, his nickname suggesting nourishment, his last name suggesting an organic metaphor related to the pear tree metaphor. Moreover, as the "son of Evening Sun" (281), thus the source of light for earth, he is figuratively the sun to Janie's pear tree. He believes in Janie's good sense, treats her as an equal, and expects that they will join in any endeavor—playing and working, cooking and hunting. Though Janie leaves Eatonville to work beside him "down on the muck" in south Florida, she chooses to do so, thus moving from Nanny's high seat, from Jody's prestigious porch, from the house to the fields to work as she had sworn to Logan Killicks she'd never do. Most important, Tea Cake encourages her to join in the life there—the laughter, the language contests, the stories, and the rich, full experiences of her people. Loving Tea Cake is the catalyst that helps transform Janie from the dead to the living. In fact, when Janie realizes for the first time that Tea Cake does love her, "she was lit up like a transfiguration" (159).

Living with Tea Cake, Janie finds a great romantic love as well as love and pride in her race, but she also experiences hard work in the fields, disaster in the hurricane and its accompanying flood, and the painful circumstances surrounding Tea Cake's death. From the garden through the flood and death, with all the obvious archetypal resonances, Janie moves through the cycle of most of humankind's possibilities.

Finishing the story of her life in past tense, Janie ends the novel speaking in the present tense to Pheoby, the same way she began it. As she discusses her present circumstances, the major patterns of imagery collaborate to reinforce them. In her own description of her life, the pear tree has matured, is no longer limited to the sexual, but has become a part of the universal cycle of living things from birth to death. "Janie saw her life like a great tree in leaf with the things suffered, things enjoyed, things done and undone. Dawn and doom was in the branches" (20).

Her spiritual growth has allowed her to be "a delegate to de big 'ssociation of life, to the 'big convention of livin' " (18). Indeed she insists she has "been tuh de horizon and back" (284). She has returned to live alone, her life not dependent on anyone else. As she mounts the stairs to her bedroom, "the light in her hand was like a spark of sun-stuff washing her face in fire" (285). Once alone there, she thinks: "Here was peace. She pulled in her horizon like a great fish-net. Pulled it in from around the waist of the world and draped it over her shoulder. So much of life in its meshes! She called in her soul to come and see" (286). All patterns of imagery coalesce. Great with life as the tree in leaf, radiant with the spark, the fire of a fully realized humanity, and shaping her horizon, her world, about her with her self as center, she calls in her soul to acknowledge the wonder. She has learned, finally, that her life is as much part of the mysterious, creative, wondrous process of the universe as the pear tree. She has now found her "personal answer" like "all other creations" (24).

Because we are aware of the connections between Hurston and Walker, we expect—and do indeed find—resemblances both in the elements making up the novels and in the theme of the novels. Celie of *The Color Purple* shares with Janie a similar background, endures similar trials, and most important for her own survival, she too attains a "sense of wonder" that allows her to remain physically undiminished.

Celie seems to be an almost deliberate delineation of the mule of the world, and apparently nothing is too brutal to be vented on her. Her ordeals, painful to discuss, leave her more dead than alive. At fourteen, writing her letters to God because there is no one else she can tell, she has been sexually abused and made pregnant twice by the man she believes to be her father; she is berated and shamed for wickedness by her dying mother, who is unaware of her husband Alphonso's guilt; and then she is forced to grieve silently as Alphonso (actually her stepfather) disposes of her two babies, either killing them or selling them, as Celie supposes.

Described by Alphonso as dumb, lying, and promiscuous, Celie, with a cow thrown in to boot, is unloaded on Albert, an older widowed man with four children. The children abuse and overwork her; Albert beats her, works her both in the house and the field, and insists on sexual accommodation, treating her meanwhile as if he can hardly bear the sight of her. Then Albert evicts Nettie, Celie's younger sister and the only person whom Celie loves and who loves Celie in return. As Nettie leaves, Celie begs only for one thing—that Nettie write if she is not dead. Nettie never writes. Deprived of anything to live for, Celie thinks of Nettie's parting injunction, that Celie must fight for life. But Nettie tried to fight and she's gone, most probably dead, so Celie chooses a different course.

Celie chooses life-in-death: to endure Albert's beatings, for instance, she chooses *not* to feel, to make herself numb, to look forward to an afterlife where, she imagines, things will be better. The final realization of nothingness descends on Celie when she learns that for all the time she has grieved over Nettie's death, Nettie has been alive and writing to Celie from Africa. Albert has simply withheld the letters. First she wants to kill Albert, but then she desires only a retreat to nothingness, to a time and place where nothing and no one exists. Celie, alive physically, has banished all emotional life except for an occasional resurgent desire to kill or maim Albert.

After Albert brings Shug Avery, his former lover, to his home to recuperate under Celie's care, life begins to stir in Celie again. Shug represents the female beauty and high spirits that Celie is starved for. But more than that, she is also the first person besides Nettie to be grateful for Celie's hard work, to praise Celie for the many skills that Celie does indeed have despite Albert's insults, and the first since Nettie to love Celie as a person. The love that develops between them is sexual and physical, but as Celie tries to explain, it resembles the love Celie felt for her mama, for Nettie, and for her lost babies too.

Shug's love, however sustaining it may be to Celie, is an exterior support; it can help but cannot give inner strength, that sense of an undiminished self that Walker so admires. In the words of Janie Crawford, "Two things everybody's got tuh do fuh theyselves. They got tuh go tuh God, and they got tuh find out about livin' fuh themselves" (285). With Shug's love, Celie is beginning to find out about living, and like Janie her soul is beginning to crawl out of its hiding place. But if in fact we assume that going to God means simply death, not acceptance of orthodox Christian salvation—and Janie's solution is certainly not orthodox—if in fact both novels view it as expanding the soul's horizons to reflect the spark of the self as an integral part of the plan of Creation, Celie has her greatest struggle still before her.

For one thing, she has come to view God as the white power structure describes Him and to view religion as a kind of fire insurance for which one barters with God. From her first letter written to God, she has expected to barter. She writes that she has been a good girl (and of course she has) and that because of this perhaps He will give her a sign letting her know what is happening to her. Believing that surely she has struck a bargain, she can neither understand nor forgive God when He does not keep what she believes is the contract. When Nettie's letters are finally returned to her, she learns that Alphonso, who raped and impregnated her, was not her real father, that her real father had been lynched because he was financially successful in the white business world; that her mother, left alone with Celie and Nettie, lost her mind after seeing her husband's charred and mutilated body and married Alphonso, who proceeded to finish destroying her. God has known all this and let her suffer agonies, so Celie writes her supposedly last letter to Him, recounting her pain and accusing God of being asleep.

Celie now comes to see God as a tall, graybearded, white man who like other men she has known does not listen to women like her. Insofar as Celie can discern, God is deaf, and He certainly has not done anything for her. Shug still argues, however, that sinner that she herself is, God loves her. Celie finds this incredible but listens carefully as Shug begins to explain.

Shug offers Celie basically Janie's philosophy of the "spark" in all humankind as a theory about God, a theory that will finally encompass even the color purple, giving the novel its title. Furthermore Shug says that God is not a she or a he but an It that doesn't look like anything. Shug urges Celie to see herself as connected to everything, to recognize that the smallest thing in the universe is meant to delight and please by suggesting to the human spirit the fullness and richness, the wonder, of Creation. Even something so small as the color purple wherever it may be found—in the color of flowers, for example, Shug adds. In response Celie says that she must revise her idea of God as an old white man and pay more attention to the wonders (corn, the color purple, etc.) God has created. But Celie is not yet ready for the color purple with its suggestions of both royalty and divinity, for she has not assumed her own importance.

Celie begins to move, gradually, toward wholeness of and reverence for the self, and begins to speak herself into existence with a spirit that surprises everyone in the family. Albert immediately begins to ridicule her, calling her black, poor, ugly, and a woman, the sum total of which, he explains, is *nothing*. In this, Albert is repeating again the words of Nanny Crawford describing the black woman as the mule of the world, the one to whom anything may be done because she is "nothing." But Celie finds a resource she has never before been aware of. As she heaps curses on Albert for his past treatment, the voice uttering maledictions does not seem to be her own, but some presence in the universe coming to her, telling her what to say and then saying it for her. Even after Shug shakes Celie to bring her from some sort of trance, the voice does not seem her own, but it speaks to everything listening. In essence, Celie acknowledges that she is black, poor, ugly, and, on top of that, she cannot cook. None of that, however, negates the fact that she exists. Celie has assumed her place in Creation.

More important, Celie must yet learn not only to enter into Creation, to say firmly "I exist," but also to maintain that philosophical stance without depending on Shug—or for that matter anyone—for assistance. Celie does have important resources to draw on, for in addition to Shug's totally independent, spirited, and free-loving attitude toward life, she has a wealth of examples of strong black women. Nettie's letters are often simply a recounting of the strength and achievements of black people in past history and in Nettie's own recent past; Sofia survives mutilation, beatings, brute labor, and an unjust prison term as a result of legal discrimination; and timid Squeak endures rape by her white uncle, the warden, when she tries to change Sofia's situation in prison. From the worst kind of degradation, all of these women insist on a place for themselves in life.

In Memphis, Celie joins their ranks, becomes confident in her abilities, and makes her own living by becoming a designer and manufacturer of pants. When Shug leaves with a new lover, a nineteen-year-old boy, Celie returns to Georgia to live in the house she inherited from her real father and contents herself with her designing among people she calls family. In her own home, she creates for herself, quite appropriately, a mostly purple room.

In her next-to-last letter, the total experience, the vital center of the novel is stated, but surprisingly the explanation comes from Albert, not Celie. Yet this too is appropriate. Shug already possessed this wisdom, Celie has proved it on her very pulses, but Albert has only recently gone through a dark night of the soul, losing every person close to him and almost his sanity. He now tells Celie that he has spent all of the recent years trying to answer the most important question about life. Why do we exist on this earth? Albert has discovered his own answer to this question, telling Celie that he believes we are here to ask questions, to ponder the big things that will lead us to answers about the little things. All this will lead inevitably to love, love of self and of the universe.

The pattern delineated in Albert's statement perfectly fits Celie's progression in her life. Her journey has ended in a sense of wonder at the magnitude and plenitude of the world, at her own place, however finite, in the scheme, at even the existence of the color purple. As a result of all this, she values herself as a part of Creation, recognizes others as subjects not objects, and then, like Albert, begins to love both self and others. In fact, she has long since forgiven Albert and feels a certain affection for him, though she refuses his proposal that they marry again. It is also true that she has not learned more about "the big things" and that she has not developed a full-blown religious system as such. But if the much repeated statement is true, that the foundation of all worship is wonder, Celie has succeeded where many fail.

When Shug writes that she is coming home, Celie decides that she will be content whether Shug is there or not. Celie thus has learned that the quality of life must not depend on externals; to be alive, to find one's worth, to rest content in the wonder—that is what the color purple signifies. Celie can surround herself in royal purple, for she is in command of a kingdom, the only proper one for humankind, one's own self.

Beyond analyzing this theme common to both novels—a similarity that neither diminishes Hurston's book by Walker's rehearsal of its theme nor makes Walker's imitative, but instead enriches both—we should no doubt ask what wisdom each book offers to oppressed women universally for dealing with the realities of their lives. It is easier perhaps to say what the novels do not attempt. Unlike self-help guidebooks, they do not offer direct and immediate advice for relieving economic, social, and political burdens. Nor are they thinly disguised religious exhortations. Celie and Janie's participation in their rather mystical experiences does not lead them, like Uncle Tom, to freedom through Christian salvation and death. They do not adopt Christian humility, piety, and submission to oppression in this world as a trade-off for happiness in the next. Their pilgrimage, from death-in-life back to life, allows them to take their places in this world by valuing themselves as part of a wondrous Creation.

Each novel may, on the other hand, offer the quality necessary for change in any area of life—for black women, for all women, for anyone who would be free. That is the assurance of worth, of value—not that which society can confer, for what can be given by it can be taken away by it—but an assurance on a cosmic level that even if mystical and unexplainable is still certain. Alice Walker, in praising the qualities of Zora Neale Hurston as a writer, says it best. Saying that no book is more important to her than *Their Eyes Were Watching God*, she goes on to name qualities in Hurston's writing that she admires most, of which the most distinctive is "a sense of black people as complete, complex, undiminished human beings." (See essay reprinted in Chapter 2 of this volume.)

Undiminished, of course, is applicable not just to Hurston's Janie but to Walker's Celie as well. If any person can recognize herself as "the world and the heavens boiled down to a drop" as each of these characters ultimately is able to do, she then realizes herself not as contributing to, but as representing Creation. As such, she cannot be diminished physically even though her worldly circumstances are demeaning, for she both is, and is part of, a wondrous Creation.

WORKS CITED

Hurston, Zora Neale. *Their Eyes Were Watching God.* Philadelphia: J. B. Lippincott, 1937; Urbana: University of Illinois Press, 1978.

Walker, Alice. *The Color Purple.* New York: Harcourt Brace Jovanovich, 1982.

—. *In Search of Our Mothers' Gardens: Womanist Prose.* New York: Harcourt Brace Jovanovich, 1983.

6

"That Which the Soul Lives By": Spirituality in the Works of Zora Neale Hurston and Alice Walker

Mary Ann Wilson

Zora Neale Hurston and Alice Walker are spiritual sisters whose lives and works affirm racial pride and beauty. Discovering in Hurston an echoing voice, Walker set out not only to find and mark her grave but, more important, to keep her spirit alive by adding to the still unfolding story of black survival and power. A necessary part of such a story is, of course, black resistance to a variety of oppressions—a resistance that always takes a creative form, whether it be sermons, letters, communal talkfests, street marches, a well-tended garden, or lovingly woven cloth. For both Hurston and Walker spiritual survival is linked to such creativity rather than to any institutional religion or system of beliefs. Seeing the creative spark in aspects of life, the two women came to believe in the spirituality of the creative process itself.

Both writers speak often of the need for black expression, the almost compulsive desire to assert a unique identity in the face of white bourgeois values. Hurston believed the black "will to adorn" was proof of the inherently dramatic nature of blacks, whether "strutting their stuff" on the street corners or transforming the pulpit into a stage. As Robert Hemenway notes, Hurston believed that "the black masses . . . triumphed over their racist environment, not by becoming white and emulating bourgeois values . . . or political propaganda, but by turning inward to create the blues, the folktale, the spiritual, the hyperbolic lie, the ironic joke" (51). Walker too cites the force of woman's creative impulse, which must express itself or degenerate into spiritual paralysis, impotent rage, or even suicide if it is denied. We think of Celie turning to piecing quilts instead of cutting Mr. __'s throat (*Color Purple* 125); or of Meridian, guilt-ridden and haunted until she accepts her role in the civil rights movement, thereby giving herself and her people a voice. As Hurston and Walker realized, unless blacks turn to something that is their own, they will be rejecting a life-giving source of identity and power.

Yet a close reading of both writers shows us characters who not only embrace their culture as a source of strength but also transcend it by creating an alternative reality either of language or action. Janie in *Their Eyes Were Watching God*, John Pearson in *Jonah's Gourd Vine*, and Celie in *The Color Purple* are examples of characters whose verbal adeptness gives them power in the black community. But both writers came to realize that language mastery is only one step in the evolution toward action—action that involves meaningful participation in the community, which in turn brings self-fulfillment and spiritual wholeness. This reaching out to the community is evident in *Their Eyes Were Watching God* and *The Color Purple*, in Hurston's and Walker's own comments about their work, and perhaps most concretely in Walker's 1976 novel, *Meridian*.

Since, as Keith Byerman notes, "for blacks questions of art are always questions of power" (2), then mastery of language confers a kind of power on those who have it, and ultimately contributes to their spiritual survival. When Janie in *Their Eyes Were Watching God* begins to break out of the imprisonment of self into which her first two marriages had plunged her, she turns to her own culture and its language, making a place for herself on the front porch of Joe Clarke's store—previously all male—and showing off to the community her verbal adeptness. She literally and figuratively creates an identity through the "new language" Tea Cake teaches her:

> Ah'm older than Tea Cake, yes. But he done showed me where it's de thought dat makes de difference in ages. If people thinks de same they can make it all right. So in the beginnin' new thoughts had tuh be thought and new words said. . . . He done taught me de maiden language all over. (173)

Hurston and Walker, knowing the power of the word in black culture, often turn to black dialect as a rich source of meaning in their works. Charting Hurston's own career as an anthropologist demonstrates this desire to tap the elemental sources of language and its expression in folklore. The clinical approach of the professional anthropologist gradually and inevitably gave way to an earthier, more elemental, study as she realized she must go back to the people and "dress as they did, talk as they [did]" (Hemenway 215) before she could understand the folklore they were creating. In true Emersonian fashion, Hurston searched for the poetry behind the language, accurately recording the rhymes and rhythms of black folklore not from the perspective of the outsider but from a communal perspective within the society she was observing. The power inherent in the black's unique response to his world—an affirmation in the face of adversity—finds its way into Hurston's novel *Jonah's Gourd Vine* in the person of John Pearson, the preacher.

In her original dedication of the novel, Hurston refers to those "first and only real Negro poets in America—the preachers, who bring barbaric splendor of word and song into the very camp of the mockers" (Hemenway 195). Projecting a control in his sermons he lacks in his personal life, John Pearson is a true folk hero, uneducated, unsophisticated, but endowed with an innate linguistic power. When he first meets his future wife Lucy, he is in awe of her because she has a command of language and a reputation in the community for her verbal facility. John's verbal skills are cruder and less educated than Lucy's, but he is in touch with the idiom of the people. He feels the crude rhymes and songs he knows are inadequate to win Lucy, so he makes up "imaginary speeches" to her—"speeches full of big words that would make her gasp and do him 'reverence' " (64–65).

Here Hurston introduces the notion of divinity as somehow connected to language and prepares us for the emergence of John later in the novel as the preacher-poet, an Emersonian wordsmith with a difference. Whereas Emerson asserts that the man who is able to use "picturesque language" is "a man in alliance with truth and God" (*Nature* 30), the opposite is true with John. He is most eloquent when he is suffering and sinful. Perhaps the conflict here lies in what Larry Neal sees as two distinct kinds of spirituality in the novel: the one, a relic of slavery, communal and non-Christian, with "no clean-cut dichotomy between the world of spirit and the world of flesh"; the other more Puritan and evangelical in its background (*Jonah's Gourd Vine* 6–7). Such a split characterizes the hybrid Christianity blacks appropriated in this country, an issue we will explore later.

Shortly after the first time Lucy finds out about his womanizing, John stands up in church and prays in the traditional black rhetorical pose of the sinner man:

> You are de same God, Ah
> Dat heard de sinner man cry.
> Same God dat sent de zigzag lightning tuh
> Join de mutterin' thunder.
> Same God dat holds de elements
> In uh unbroken chain of controllment.
> Same God dat hung on Cavalry and died,

> Dat we might have a right tuh de tree of life—
> We thank Thee that our sleeping couch
> Was not our cooling board,
> Our cover was not our winding sheet . . .
> Please tuh give us uh restin' place
> Where we can praise Thy name forever,
> Amen. (145)

His words and delivery impress the community, convert some in the congregation, and launch his vocation as preacher. Yet, as Hemenway points out, John can save others but not himself: "He is a poet who graces his world with language but cannot find the words to secure his own personal grace" (196). The power of John's language—the spiritual dimension of his creative urge—reaches out to the community but is ineffectual in his own life.

A more successful illustration of the power inherent in language and its spiritual dimension is Walker's heroine Celie in *The Color Purple*. Walker's own belief in the redemptive, healing properties of writing lies behind the creation of perhaps her most compelling character. Viewing the writing process as a "kind of visitation of spirits" (Bradley 36), Walker sees artistic expression as a means of linking human and divine nature. Significant here is that Celie begins writing letters to God, then shifts midway in the novel to Nettie, her sister, but finally comes full circle at the conclusion of the book, addressing her last letter to God, stars, trees, sky, "peoples," to everyone and everything (242).

What is crucial to an understanding of Walker's novel is the role language plays for the semiliterate Celie. It is escape and expression, but it is also a paradigm of Celie's evolution from faceless nonentity to mature sister, mother, and creator. As Byerman notes,

> Celie writes herself into humanity and thereby contradicts the stipulation that she be a mere cipher. She gives herself an inner life and a concrete history and thus an otherness that the patriarchal order denies her. (163)

Galvanized into being by the creative act of writing, Celie survives an incredible series of dehumanizing experiences, maintaining a tenuous grip on sanity despite her suffering. Even the fact that Celie's letters to Nettie come back to her in an unopened packet finally seems inconsequential in light of the power the very act of writing them has conferred on Celie. The order and control lacking in her own life, the voice denied her by her repressive environment, surfaces in these documents of her survival. Yet Celie's voice is not merely a written one, for her linguistic power builds throughout the novel to the climactic scene where, like a conjure woman, she hurls curses at Mr. __ (see *Color Purple* 176).

In the last phrases of this pivotal speech, Walker suggests that the strength and power Celie feels come from a source outside herself, a spiritual realm recalling the author's mystical approach to language. The artist, the creator, is in touch with an Emersonian, transcendent world of meaning where language confers a spiritual power over self and the world. Unlike John Pearson's eloquent though hollow sermonizing in *Jonah's Gourd Vine*, Celie's words save her.

A closer look at Hurston and Walker, however, shows that frequently words alone are not enough. The spiritual, redemptive dimension of the creative process can and often must manifest itself not only through language but through action. The dramatic quality in black life that Hurston notes demands public expression and, more crucially, community validation. Both writers believe intensely that the community plays a vital role in black culture: a central factor in John Pearson's failure as a man is ultimately his failure in the eyes of the community to live up to their ideal of the preacher; Janie Starks's gradual evolution into a vibrant, three-dimensional woman is not complete until she both plays her linguistic role among the men on Joe Clarke's porch and reenters the community her previous two husbands had denied her; Celie's spiritual odyssey, begun through her letter writing, ends when she becomes a creative, productive member of the community as head of her own business, Folkspants, Unlimited.

What seems to be necessary to Hurston and Walker from the folk culture is some recognition and acknowledgment of individual worth. Indeed, critics like Frederick Karl have seen this looking outward for spiritual meaning as typical of the black woman's search for identity. Karl notes that while most white female novelists "attempt to locate the female identity in the individual, the black woman seeks verification also in relationships to others." (422).

Hurston's *Their Eyes Were Watching God* portrays Janie Starks from the outset as isolated from community. In her foreword to the novel, Sherley Williams characterizes Janie as "raised . . . in the white folks' yard, elevated above the common run of black people and separated from the sustenance that the community provides" (xi). In her first marriage to Logan Killicks, a wealthy farmer, Janie is kept from playing an active role in the community by Killicks's dehumanizing concept of her as a workhorse. Killicks feels his duty is to feed and to clothe Janie; providing for her material needs, he reasons, entitles him to her eternal gratitude. He takes pleasure in reminding her of her isolation:

> "Youse powerful independent around here sometime considerin'."
> "Considerin' whut for instance?"
> "Considerin' youse born in a carriage 'thout no top to it, and yo' mama and you bein' born and raised in de white folks back-yard." (51)

Janie's spiritual deprivation persists throughout their marriage until the appearance of Joe Starks and what she thinks will be the beginning of a new life. But she merely exchanges one type of isolation for another.

To Joe Starks she is a queen, too high and mighty to associate with the common folk: "Jody told her to dress up and stand in the store all that evening. Everybody was coming sort of fixed up, and he didn't mean for nobody else's wife to rank with her. She must look on herself as the bell-cow, the other women were the gang" (66). When Joe becomes mayor and the townspeople want a speech from "Mrs. Mayor Starks," Joe refuses to let her speak, and he consistently denies her a voice. Such forced separation leads Janie to realize the spiritual void in her life resulting from her marriage: "She slept with authority and so she was part of it in the town mind. She couldn't get but so close to most of them in spirit" (74). She is denied access to a vital part of her spiritual identity, as the communal recognition and acceptance she seeks elude her.

When Joe Starks dies, Janie reflects wistfully on the pattern her life should have taken:

> She had been getting ready for her great journey to the horizons in search of people; it was important to all the world that she should find them and they find her. (138)

Tea Cake Woods allows Janie to find the people, to gain the sense of community she craved. Working beside him in the "muck" of the Florida Everglades, Janie mingles with the workers, male and female, laughs, jokes, and learns to tell a good story. She is a part of the rich creative life of the folk, even in their time of suffering. Waiting out the hurricane near the end of the novel, in a scene emblematic of black communal response, Janie feels connected to "the others in other shanties, their eyes straining against crude walls and their souls asking if He meant to measure their puny might against His" (236). Speaking up in her own defense later in the novel, Janie wins grudging forgiveness of this same community for having killed Tea Cake, "because they really loved Janie just a little less than they had loved Tea Cake." (282).

The novel finally comes full circle in the closing pages when Hurston reminds us it has been a story told by the returning Janie "to Pheoby . . . her best friend and the symbolic representative of the community" (Christian, "Trajectories" 175). Pheoby perhaps speaks for the community when, after hearing Janie's story, she exclaims: "Ah done growed ten feet higher from jus' listenin' tuh you, Janie. Ah ain't satisfied wid mahself no mo' " (284). Janie has returned to the people as spokeswoman for a life many of them only dream of. But she has lived it.

The same determination that leads black writers like Hurston and Walker to affirm the strength and viability of black culture also causes them to adopt a unique black Christianity emblematic of the black response to Judeo-Christian tradition. Such reworking and rethinking of white Christianity ultimately derives, as Trudier Harris notes, from the folk culture many blacks cling to. The subversion of traditional religious beliefs becomes as necessary for survival as the creative impulse and is, in fact, yet another manifestation of the black creative response to life. As Harris notes:

> Folk creations allowed for a broader glimpse into the workings of human nature. Usually they encouraged interactions on levels of mutual humanity and respect instead of the master/slave relationship which Christianity supported. (53)

Hemenway, too, notes the black view of slavery as a system sanctioned by the hypocrisy of white Christianity (224). By creating an alternative version of traditional religious belief, blacks thus affirm their heritage in folk tradition and assert a basically universalist vision of the world.

Such an apparently radical re-visioning of Christianity resembles the reaction of mid-nineteenth-century transcendentalism to the cool formalism of Puritan beliefs. Rejecting codified notions of divinity, Emerson argued for an immanent God ever present in his creation and intuited from it—the God Celie comes to know and love in Shug and the natural world, or Hurston sees in Janie: "the world and the heavens boiled down to a drop" (*Their Eyes* 119). Emerson called for a democratization of the religious experience, urged us all to "enjoy an original relation to the universe," saying: "All that Adam had, all that Caesar could, you have and can do" (*Nature* 3, 76). The only obstacle to vital religious experience is one of vision: "The ruin or blank that we see when we look at nature, is in our own eye. The axis of vision is not coincident with the axis of things, and so they appear not transparent but opaque" (*Nature* 73). But nature is there "to conspire with spirit to emancipate us" (*Nature* 50). Similarly, Hurston and Walker believe that the spiritual redemption of blacks demands that they first see beyond the white man's anthropomorphic concept of deity and open themselves to a more universalist principle of divinity permeating all matter.

Because of her brutalization at the hands of the men in her life, Celie in *The Color Purple* envisions God as a "He." She feels alienated in the face of the old white man of the Bible, the cold and indifferent Jehovah who presides over the ubiquitous suffering that afflicts her and her people; still, she recognizes that she needs "something," that agnosticism is not the answer. Shug suggests an alternative: First, stop thinking about God as Man. Celie must reconstitute her "axis of vision," and as her sister Nettie discovers in Africa, intuit the presence of God as an immanent force alive equally in her fellow man and woman and in the work of "His" hands—such as the color purple in a field of violets. Animism, of course, was part of the black pre-Christian religious experience and is, according to Walker, one of the elements African-Americans have retained of their heritage. It is this receptivity to kindred spirit in all matter that enables her black characters to reconcile the Emersonian "Me" and "Not Me" and to achieve spiritual health.

The universalist concept of God as spirit focuses one's vision on humanity and a secular salvation. In her autobiography, *Dust Tracks on a Road*, Zora Neale Hurston witnesses divinity not in codified doctrine or institutional structures but in the tangible manifestations of man's creative spirit:

> If I have not felt the divinity of man in his cults, I have found it in his works. When I lift my eyes to the towering structures of Manhattan, and look upon the mighty tunnels and bridges of the world, I know that my search is over and that I can depart in peace. (323)

Shug tells Celie in *The Color Purple* that we come to church not to find God but to share him (165). Shug forges her way back to the world in the art of singing; a major aspect of Celie's self-discovery is likewise her artistic self-expression, not only through the letters she writes to God and later to Nettie but through the hundreds of pants she sews for family, friends, and the public. When Celie discovers her husband has kept all Nettie's letters from her, her first impulse is to kill him. But Shug admonishes her to sew pants instead and to forget about killing. The creative impulse gives direction to Celie's spiritual energies, saves her from the murderous, putting a needle instead of a razor in her hand.

The creativity of black women is a favorite theme for Alice Walker because it involves salvaging a future from what one critic calls the "horror and waste" of many women's lives (Christian, *Black Women* 212). Walker's works suggest that "if women cannot fulfill their nature, the creative spirit within them, they become dangerous, catatonic, or paralyzed by guilt" (Christian, *Black Women* 252). And since the black woman's identity is tied so intricately to the community, she must channel her anger and rage at the world into constructive avenues that will yield something tangible for others to judge and evaluate. Shug is not only a strong woman but a creative one. Her singing is proof. Celie, too, must begin to construct an identity—to be someone—through what she can make (what Emerson would call "commodity"). The few pairs of pants she sews for friends and relatives gradually become Folkspants, Unlimited, her own company.

When she begins to sew, Celie turns out not assembly-line clothes, but pants uniquely suited to the personalities of those she loves. Her gratitude to Shug emerges in the beauty of the cloth she chooses for her pants. Her love and respect for Odessa's husband, Jack, lives in the soft, strong camel-colored pants she creates for him. Celie's slow healing process, her peacemaking with the world, is the beautiful succession of clothes that comes from her hands. Emerson's essay "The Poet" yields an interesting commentary on such latent creativity, for he feels "the man is only half himself, the other half is his expression" (*Early Lectures* 349).

In her 1976 novel, *Meridian*, Alice Walker explores the tension between two dichotomous forms of religious experience open to the black community: one, focused on the other world, reinforces a master-slave mentality and renders its followers docile and calloused to the needs of suffering humanity; the other directs its followers toward humanity and into constructive activity designed to achieve spiritual and material liberation.

An intensely spiritual young woman, idealistic and confused by the incendiary rhetoric of her 1960s contemporaries, Meridian at first rejects the church she identifies with her mother's generation. The comfort it gives is false in her eyes because it leads to a complacency and spiritual blindness to the needs of humanity. Eyes fixed on heaven miss the pathos and beauty of this world. Meridian associates the church with apathy and passivity, seeing how it has lulled her mother into a mindless acceptance of incomprehensible sermons and second-class citizenship.

The church her mother has accepted is narrow and constricting; what Meridian needs is a more vital earth-centered church responsive to the political and social needs of her people. The compassion Meridian's father feels for the dispossessed Indians her mother finds incomprehensible, as she later fails to understand Meridian's part in black voter registration drives and civil rights marches. Like the prayer pillows she makes too small for kneeling, Mrs. Hill's religion is pointless and impractical because it lacks a human dimension. Meridian gradually realizes the church she needs must have this dimension, must lead her not to cast her eyes toward heaven but to see God in suffering humanity.

Yet Meridian is restless, unsatisfied, still craving something more than the social gospel she has lived by. Near the end of the novel she begins going back to church, first one, then another, as she looks for the wholeness she lacks. What she discovers, as one critic notes, is a sense of church that is all-encompassing, communal (Parker-Smith 488).What has held congregations through the years is the ancient music that holds Meridian now—"the song of the people," experienced, transformed, and then passed down from generation to generation. Paradoxically, Meridian experiences a spiritual rebirth because, as a lover of humanity, she has finally acknowledged a vital part of her people's worship—the ritual—that she has previously ignored.

The spirituality of Janie Starks, Meridian, or Celie amounts to a "womanizing" (Walker's term) of the transcendental ethic. While Hurston's and Walker's place in the canon of black women writers is secure, perhaps we should see them also in the context of mainstream American writers like Emerson and Whitman. Both women argue for Emerson's original relationship to the universe, an active, aggressive, confrontational approach that leads them to view the dialect and folkways of blacks as art. A mutual preoccupation with the spiritual survival of their people leads both writers to explore art and religion as spiritual affirmations of a whole people, complementary routes to the same destination. In an ethos beyond the confines of church or ideology, the religious and the aesthetic manifest a similar "will to adorn."

The quilt motif that appears so frequently in *The Color Purple* is an apt metaphor of the network of human lives Alice Walker believes must and can eventually save us. Fit together over the years from pieces of clothing the family owned, symbolizing both the continuity of generations and the fragmented past of the black race, the quilt is an artifact taken up in time of pain and suffering. It is, along with the unflinchingly honest letters Celie writes, her overture to the world. In a symbolic gesture, Celie gives the quilt to Sofia when Sofia leaves her obtuse husband, Harpo—observing their kinship in the pattern of the quilt, appropriately named "Sister's Choice."

Hurston and Walker never lose sight of this world; they look not for an externally imposed God or religion but at a divinity arising from interaction with nature, community, and self. Such an earth-rooted vision characterizes the spirituality of Zora Neale Hurston and Alice Walker.

WORKS CITED

Bradley, David. "Novelist Alice Walker: Telling the Black Woman's Story." *The New York Times Magazine*, January 8, 1984, pp. 25–37.

Byerman, Keith E. *Fingering the Jagged Grain: Tradition and Form in Recent Black Fiction*. Athens: University of Georgia Press, 1985.

Christian, Barbara. *Black Women Novelists: The Development of a Tradition, 1892–1976*. Westport, Conn.: Greenwood Press, 1980.

——. "Trajectories of Self-Definition: Placing Contemporary Afro-American Women's Fiction." In *Black Feminist Criticism: Perspectives on Black Women Writers*, 171–186. New York: Pergamon Press, 1985.

Emerson, Ralph Waldo. *The Early Lectures of Ralph Waldo Emerson, 1838–1842*. Vol. 3. Edited by Robert E. Spiller and Wallace E. Williams. Cambridge, Mass.: Harvard University Press, 1972.

——. *Nature: Addresses and Lectures*. Boston: Houghton-Mifflin, 1903; New York: AMS Press, 1968.

Harris, Trudier. "Three Black Women Writers and Humanism: A Folk Perspective." In *Black American Literature and Humanism*, edited by R. Baxter Miller, 50–74. Lexington: University of Kentucky Press, 1981.

Hemenway, Robert E. *Zora Neale Hurston: A Literary Biography*. Urbana: University of Illinois Press, 1977.

Hurston, Zora Neale. *Dust Tracks on a Road: An Autobiography*. Philadelphia: J. B. Lippincott, 1942; Urbana: University of Illinois Press, 1971, 1984.

——. *Jonah's Gourd Vine*. Philadelphia: J. B. Lippincott, 1934, 1971.

——. *Mules and Men*. Philadelphia: J. B. Lippincott, 1935; Bloomington: Indiana University Press, 1963, 1978.

——. *Their Eyes Were Watching God*. Philadelphia: J. B. Lippincott, 1937; Urbana: University of Illinois Press, 1978.

Karl, Frederick R. *American Fictions 1940–1980: A Comprehensive History and Critical Evaluation*. New York: Harper & Row, 1983.

O'Brien, John, ed. *Interviews with Black Writers*. New York: Liveright, 1973.

Parker-Smith, Bettye J. "Alice Walker's Women: In Search of Some Peace of Mind." In *Black Women Writers (1950–1980): A Critical Evaluation*, edited by Mari Evans, 478–493. Garden City, N.Y.: Anchor Press/Doubleday, 1984.

Walker, Alice. *The Color Purple*. New York: Harcourt Brace Jovanovich, 1982.

——. *In Search of Our Mothers' Gardens: Womanist Prose*. New York: Harcourt Brace Jovanovich, 1983.

——. *Meridian*. New York: Harcourt, Brace, 1976; New York: Pocket Books/Simon & Schuster, 1976.

7

Redemption Through Redemption of the Self in *Their Eyes Were Watching God* and *The Color Purple*

Emma J. Waters Dawson

Writing in an essay, "Saving the Life That Is Your Own," Alice Walker pays homage to Zora Neale Hurston and other black women writers as people whose experiences she had to get to know, imbibe, and then pass on (*In Search* 9). Walker cites Zora Neale Hurston as having perhaps the greatest influence on her craft. Both writers mined literary material from southern soil: Hurston emphasized the Eatonville, Florida, milieu as a main setting; Walker often utilizes a rural setting in Georgia as the background for her fiction. The South, therefore, provides for both writers a spiritual balance and an ideological base from which to construct their characters.

A persistent characteristic found in both writers is their use of a southern African-American woman as the protagonist and that character's insistence on challenging convention, on being herself. Inherent in the fiction of both is a black feminine bent (Walker prefers the term womanist), variously manifested in their depiction of dilemmas caused by conflicting ideologies about women, in their prescription of a course of action for women that is antithetical to accepted masculine views, or in their formulation of a synthesis between racial and sexual discrimination as a norm for human oppression (Royster 98). Reflecting their concern with the self, Hurston in 1937 wrote *Their Eyes Were Watching God* and Walker, in 1982, *The Color Purple*.

Walker in *The Color Purple* builds upon the black female characterizations present in *Their Eyes Were Watching God*. Hurston becomes an invaluable role model for her in that Walker adapts to her own needs Hurston's depiction of individual and group suffering by black women.

In both *Their Eyes Were Watching God* and *The Color Purple*, black women suffer stressful situations: loveless, dull marriages, stifled creativity, jealous or cruel spouses, sexual and racial victimization, capitulation to ignorance and tradition, and myriad other problems. Yet, in both novels the black female protagonist's principal source of strength appears to be the knowledge, gained through experience, that suffering seems the maternal legacy of the African-American woman, and that survival is effective revenge for the pain.

The female protagonists, Janie in Hurston's novel and Celie in *The Color Purple*, both possess the potential for creativity. The oppression of sex, race, or class stifles or thwarts their artistic potential. Nevertheless, these women manage to realize their artistic potential, often encouraged by the sharing of their experiences within a network of female nurturance. Despite the circumstances that oppress the women characters in *Their Eyes Were Watching God* and *The Color Purple*, they survive through their re-creation of the self.

In her essay "In Search of Our Mothers' Gardens," Walker speaks about three types of black women: the physically and psychologically abused black women, the black women who are torn by contrary instincts, and the new black woman, who re-creates herself out of the creative legacy of her maternal ancestors (*In Search* 235–238). These types are present in Walker's fiction today, but significantly, Hurston also utilizes these types as images in *Their Eyes Were Watching God* and establishes herself as a literary model in her creation of characters. Both Janie and her grandmother, Nanny, are vivid images of physically and psychologically abused black women.

The first important influence that Janie remembers is Nanny, who bequeaths to her granddaughter the conception of women in slavery (Rosenblatt 88–89). This inherited conception from a patriarchal and racist society functions as an obstacle to Janie's potential to realize her creativity. Nanny's attitudes toward men, marriage, love, and life grew out of her experiences as a slave woman. Lloyd W. Brown sees Nanny as "actually quite faithful to those very caste systems (race, sex, and money) which have restrictively defined her own past and which seem so intrinsic to the situation of the black woman in America as a whole and in the rural South in particular" (42). Because of the legacy of psychological abuse Nanny passes on to Janie, she is determined to see that her granddaughter is not misused as she and her daughter have been in a patriarchal and racist society. Lorraine Bethel sees in this cross-generational relationship the pattern of black women's victimization by oppressive racial and sexual forces. In this sense, "Janie and her grandmother illustrate the tragic continuity of black female oppression in white/male America" (182).

Nanny reveals the depth of this continuity of oppression when she channels Janie's adolescence into constricting social conformity by arranging a marriage with middle-aged, prosperous Logan Killicks. When Janie objects because she does not love a man she barely knows, Nanny speaks about the impracticality and irrelevance of romance in the life of the African-American woman:

> Lawd have mussy! Dat's de very prong all us black women gits hung on. Dis love! Dat's just whut's got us uh pullin' and uh haulin' and sweatin' and doin' from can't see in de mornin' till can't see at night. Dat's how come de ole folks say dat bein' uh fool don't kill nobody. It jus' makes you sweat. (*Their Eyes* 41)

In her tirade, Nanny ironically acknowledges the paradoxical role love has traditionally played in the life of the African-American woman, for her own life experiences as a slave and as a freed woman have denied her the right to perpetuate her sexual relations and family life in the way she may have liked. Nevertheless, she attempts to force Janie to conform to how she may have desired her own life to be.

In contrast to Nanny, Janie is torn by contrary instincts and actually is inspired by the creative impulse. Her transformation, despite opposition, of the bits and pieces allowed her by a racist and sexist society into a work of functional beauty begins during adolescence when watching a pear tree blossom, she is stirred by strange wonderings: "A blossoming pear tree had called her to come and gaze on a mystery" (23). As a female protagonist functioning in romantic and sensual love, Janie

> saw a dust bearing bee sink into the sanctum of a bloom, the thousand sister-calyxes arch to meet the love embrace and the ecstatic shiver of the tree from root to tiniest branch creaming in every blossom and frothing with delight. So this was a marriage! She had been summoned to behold a revelation. (24)

The orgasmic imagery of the blossoming pear tree that Janie witnesses and equates with marriage between a man and a woman represents the initial stirrings of creativity in her life. The image of the pear tree becomes a catalyst for her to realize her creative potential. Perhaps, with her vivid imagination, in another place or time, Janie might have become an artist or writer.

In this scene, Hurston advocates the full expression of one's mental, physical, sexual, and creative abilities. Janie "was seeking confirmation of the voice and vision, and everywhere she found and acknowledged answers. A personal answer for all other creations except herself" (24). Moreover, Hurston establishes here the potential for the emergence of the third type of woman Walker discusses, the new black woman who re-creates herself out of the creative legacy of her maternal ancestors.

Idealistically dreaming of love and beauty in her search for a man, Janie reveals the potential for creativity in her life. Instead, she comes to the end of her childhood when Nanny catches her at sixteen kissing "no good" Johnny Taylor across the gatepost. Nanny responds by rushing Janie into an unwanted, loveless marriage that is contrary to Janie's romantic instincts and creative vision. The young woman now begins a life in which she exemplifies the second type of woman Walker discusses, the woman torn by contrary instincts. This life continues through her second marriage to Jody Starks.

Threatened with subjugation and the stifling or thwarting of her creativity, Janie undergoes much degradation, forced acquiescence to stereotyped beliefs, and actual punishment. Yet, Janie endures, holds on to decency and sense, and triumphs in the face of apparent defeat. Later, after a third marriage that puts her on the journey to self-liberation, she returns to Eatonville to face the mob and tell her story. Sharing her story with her best friend, Pheoby, she begins a network of female nurturance. At this point in her life, Janie is representative of the new black woman who re-creates herself out of Nanny's legacy to "preach a sermon."

Janie's story proves to be quite revealing and insightful as she analyzes the events of her life and relates them to Pheoby. In doing so, she redeems herself from a stifled creativity and thus re-creates herself via the available source of art in her life. For Janie, it is storytelling. She assimilates the earlier experiences of her grandmother, mother, and of herself, studies them, and tells of them to Pheoby.

In telling Nanny's experiences of racism and sexism, Janie recognizes that her grandmother's story and her own are similar. Both women have been victimized by a patriarchal and racist society. However, in telling Pheoby that she herself has "been a delegate to de big 'ssociation of life . . . De Grand Lodge, de big convention of living (18), Janie indicates that her life has taken a path different from that of Nanny. She tells her friend that Nanny was born during slavery; therefore, it wasn't for her to fulfill her "dreams of whut a woman oughta be and to do." Still, Janie remembers Nanny's admonition: "Nothing can't stop you from wishin'. You can't beat nobody down so low till you can rob' em of they will" (31). According to

Janie's creative analysis of her own and Nanny's life, it is the combined experiences of both that helped her to shape her womanhood and individuality. It is from these experiences that Janie acknowledges that she has redeemed herself by re-creating herself through introspection and storytelling.

For Janie, the most important aspect of marriage, consistent with her potential for creativity, should be romantic love rather than economic security. Such a viewpoint contrasts sharply with that of Killicks, Janie's first husband. Thus, he becomes to her a "vision . . . desecrating the pear tree" (23). Because he fails to meet her idealistic vision of beauty and love in a marriage, he is a man contrary to her romantic instincts.

Subsequently, Janie conveys to Killicks that he fails to fulfill her expectations of a husband. Her image of him with his shovel "looking like a black bear doing some clumsy dance on his hind legs" (52) indicates not only Janie's discontent with Killicks, but also her artistic attempt to cope with a situation that is contrary to her instincts. As an aspiring artist, she thinks and speaks in metaphors.

In an attempt to redeem herself from oppression, Janie begins to question and challenge Killicks's exercise of power when he demands that she help him plant potatoes. If his demands that Janie help him with the planting fail to prove adequately his view of Janie as a mule, a workhorse, or slave, then his ultimate plan to buy a mule gentle enough for her so that she may assist him in the plowing does actualize Nanny's metaphor of the mule and is contrary to her romantic instincts. Aware of her sexual bondage, threatened physical abuse, and actual psychological abuse, Janie is chained to a husband and home that do not fulfill her romantic vision of finding "a bee for her bloom" (54). Not only does she feel unfulfilled as a woman, but her potential for creativity is stifled.

Janie manifests further creativity when her aspirations of love for Killicks finally turn to contempt and hate. She discovers that her potential for creativity is stifled in her forced marriage for security; unless she abandons this first loveless marriage and attempts to redeem herself she will suffer psychological abuse in a relationship contrary to her romantic instincts. "The familiar people and things had failed her so she hung over the gate and looked up the road toward way off. She knew now that marriage did not make love. Janie's first dream was dead" (44).

In deserting Killicks for a second marriage with Joe Starks, Janie prescribes for herself a course of action that is antithetical to accepted masculine views. Apparently, she instinctively feels that there is still the potential to fulfill her creative vision. However, in a second marriage for affection, she wins social position, wealth, and prestige.

Joe, Janie's second husband, acts like Mr. Washburn, Nanny's employer, in his aggressiveness and assertiveness. His language and talk appeal to Janie's romantic vision, but she, full of vivid imagery, questions whether he will "represent sunup and pollen and blooming trees" (50). Nevertheless, he does offer a change from the psychological abuse of Killicks, and seemingly provides the opportunity for her to realize her creative vision. Janie, therefore, willingly takes the chance because with Jody she desires to have "flower dust and springtime sprinkled over everything" (54).

Joe and Janie, however, cannot be equal partners in marriage, for he plans to be "a big ruler of things with her reaping the benefits" (49–50). He makes this point clear on their arrival at their new home in Eatonville. When the town unanimously selects Starks as its first mayor and one of the men calls upon Janie for a speech, Joe declares: "Mah wife don't know nothin' bout speech-makin. Ah never married her for nothin' lak dat. She's uh woman and her place is in de home" (39). Janie's inability to laugh at Joe's statement indicates her dissatisfaction at this initial state of their marriage, which is contrary to her instincts. Furthermore, Joe's statement stifles any potential for speechmaking that Janie may have possessed.

Janie asserts her potential for creative speechmaking when she compliments Joe on buying an overworked mule to allow it rest:

> Jody, dat wuz uh mighty fine thing fuh you tuh do. Tain't everybody would have thought of it, 'cause it ain't no everyday thought. Freein' dat mule makes uh mighty big man outa you. Something like George Washington and Lincoln. Abraham Lincoln, he had de whole United States tuh rule so he freed de Negroes. You got uh town so you freed uh mule. You have tuh have power tuh free things and dat makes you lak uh king uh something. (91–92)

The men obviously dismiss the irony apparent in Janie's accolade, for Hambo says, "Yo' wife is uh born orator, Starks. Us never knowed dat befo'. She put jus' de right words tuh our thoughts." It is true that the town is unaware of Janie's potential creative power in speechmaking, for Joe, believing that women should play a subordinate role in human affairs, attempts to stifle it.

Janie's awareness of Joe's intended subordination of her causes her to feign submissiveness to him:

> She found that she had a host of thoughts she had never expressed to him, and numerous emotions she had never let Jody know about.

> Things packed up and put away in parts of her heart where he could never find them. She was saving up feelings for some man she had never seen. She had an inside and an outside and suddenly she knew how not to mix them. (113)

Janie's behavior here certainly manifests a woman who acts contrary to her romantic instincts. Her instincts are to achieve her adolescent romantic vision, but Joe attempts to stifle or thwart any creativity that Janie may possess because of his preconceptions about the roles of men and women.

To cope within this masquerade of a marriage, Janie creatively masks herself in order to save her true self and preserve her romantic vision: "She sat and watched the shadow of herself going about tending store and prostrating before Jody, while all the time she herself sat under a shade tree with the wind blowing through her hair and her clothes . . . making summertime out of lonesomeness" (119). Her thoughts and her will, according to Nanny's idea, are not only part of the creative legacy left her by her maternal ancestor, but also are the bits and pieces allowed her by a sexist and racist society; therefore, she fashions them into a work of functional beauty. "It was like a drug. In a way it was good because it reconciled her to things" (119).

In her creative vision of her true self, Janie redeems herself from a stifled potential for creativity and thus re-creates herself into a new black woman. Unlike Nanny, she fashions her thoughts and her will into speechmaking or often envisions idealistic images in order to cope with unhappiness. An unequal exercise of power, reinforced by sexist oppression that stifles Janie's creativity, proves to be a source of marital conflict for both partners, and ultimately, functions as an obstacle in Janie's quest to attain her romantic vision. When material wealth and prominence prove unsatisfying, Janie searches for real values.

Thus, after Jody's death, Janie seeks and finds, in her third marriage to Vergible (Tea Cake) Woods, a love relationship between acknowledged equals. Sharing resources, work, decisions, and dangers—as well as the marriage bed—with Tea Cake, Janie finds joy, love, happiness, and adventure. She fulfills her quest with Tea Cake because he is her romantic vision: "He looked like the love thoughts of women. He could be a bee to a blossom—a pear tree blossom in the spring. He seemed to be crushing scent out of the world with his footsteps" (161). Twelve years her junior, a man of easy, engaging ways, Tea Cake brings into Janie's life the joy and companionship she was unable to realize before him.

Now representative of the new black woman who re-creates herself, Janie resists the neighbors' scorn of her effort to satisfy her romantic vision with Tea Cake. A penniless gambler, Tea Cake teaches her how to play checkers and how to drive a car; they go digging for worms by lamplight and set out for fishing after midnight. Janie's adventures with Tea Cake help complete her re-creation of the self because, for the first time in her life, she refuses to conform to the dictates of others. Aware that her soul needs freedom and experience, not security, power, and wealth, the new, self-assertive woman leaves Eatonville in a relationship that, according to Janie, "ain't no business proposition, and no race after property and titles. Dis is uh love game. Ah done lived Grandma's way. Now Ah aims tuh live mine" (171). Her departure with Tea Cake constitutes a rebellion against old and accepted standards of conduct. Not only is Janie's loving a young man a form of rebellion, but also, her marrying a man with no visible means of security places her "outside tradition" (Gayle 236). Janie re-creates herself in reality as well as in thoughts.

Although Tea Cake may be seen as representative of a romantic ideal, he, indeed, is the romantic reality, the visible evidence of her potential for creativity. He is the romantic vision that Janie has imagined, dreamed of, and searched for. Sharing responsibility with her, adapting to Janie's new definition of the female role, and creating a spirit of democracy in their marriage, Tea Cake provides Janie with spiritual fulfillment because there is no psychological abuse or operation of contrary instincts in their relationship.

Their Eyes Were Watching God depicts all three types of black women that Walker refers to in her essay. Janie's experiences as a physically and psychologically abused woman and as a woman torn by contrary instincts culminate in the new black woman who re-creates herself out of the creative legacy of her maternal ancestors. Transformed from a dreamer to a realist, Janie discovers that love affirms. She also discovers after she kills in self-defense the man she loves—the symbol of her romantic vision—that the memory of love releases her from the resultant deadness in herself. "Too busy feeling grief to dress like grief" (281), she returns to Eatonville, dressed in overalls, still revealing her womanly features, to tell her story.

Because the mob cannot approach or understand the love Tea Cake and Janie shared, Janie tells Pheoby to explain to them that love differs for every person. Comparing love to the sea and reflecting her continuous potential for creativity, Janie tells her friend: "It's uh moving thing, but still and all, it takes its shape from de shore it meets, and it's different with every shore" (284).

Pheoby's reaction to the story—"Nobody better not criticize yuh in mah hearin' " (284)—gives Janie much dignity and stature. As a result of hearing Janie's story, Pheoby plans to change her life with her husband by insisting that he take her fishing with him. Her proposal significantly shows the value the network of black female nurturance has within the community. Her action expresses the possibility that a community of women may attain redemption of the self through acting together. Now that Pheoby knows Janie's experiences, she plans to assimilate them, since Janie has become for her, and perhaps in time for the mob as well, a model in behavior, in growth of spirit and intellect that enriches and enlarges her own existence. Whereas Nanny passes on her experiences to Janie along generational lines, Janie shares her adventures with Pheoby in a woman-to-woman situation. Pheoby will convey Janie's experiences, as well as her appreciative response, to the rest of the women in the community. They may, in turn, profit from the listening and seek, as Pheoby declares, to re-create themselves.

Through Janie, Hurston creates a literary model whose life she shapes into socially meaningful patterns by exploring the psyche of the black woman while successfully dramatizing themes of genuine universal significance. With the distinction of being the first American author to explore realistically the psyche of an African-American female character, Zora Neale Hurston began a literary tradition that Alice Walker knows, assimilates, and enlarges in *The Color Purple*.

Indeed, a prolific and imaginative artist, Alice Walker has within a relatively short span of time become a touchstone in African-American literature. *The Color Purple*, for which Walker received the 1983 Pulitzer Prize for fiction, bears vivid testimony to the literary legacy that Walker has adapted from Zora Neale Hurston. By weaving taboo subjects and life styles, such as incest and lesbianism, into a creative literary pattern, Walker not only points out black women's physical and psychological abuse and black women torn by contrary instincts, she also affirms, like Hurston, her belief in personal, spiritual redemption that may evolve through the self.

Surely, Janie in *Their Eyes Were Watching God* and Celie in *The Color Purple* are sister spirits who attempt redemption through re-creation of the self. Yet, Walker adapts the classic American stock situation of rags to riches and aligns it realistically with subjects of abuse, incest, and lesbianism to affirm her creative vision that positive change, rebirth, and spiritual beauty may emerge from misery and suffering.

In probing these subjects, Walker utilizes the epistolary form. Its technique of carrying the narrative forward by letters written by one or more of the characters allows the author artistically to weave loose ends together. Unanswered questions are answered, and puzzling riddles are solved. Whereas Janie, an initially naive narrator, tells her story to her best friend, Pheoby, Celie talks with childlike innocence to God about events whose implications are too tragic or horrible to relate to anyone else. From Celie's vivid narration of a forced sexual act, the reader sees Walker's construction of the female protagonist's entrapment in an apparently inescapable, vicious cycle of abuse.

Celie's narration of rape vividly illustrates not only Walker's depiction of physical and psychological abuse, but also the plight of a young girl torn by contrary instincts (see *The Color Purple* 3). The epistolary form Walker utilizes allows the reader to be inside Celie's head as she records and comments on events. Celie reveals her emotional and psychological distress at sexual relations with the man she assumes to be her father. This abnormal dimension of sex is both objectionable and repulsive to Celie. In the absence of human warmth and after her father's warning to tell no one, she pours out her physical and psychological abuse in one letter after another. The letters reveal the apparent hopelessness of her life as well as a situation that is contrary to her instincts. Therefore, Celie represents simultaneously the first two types of oppressed black women that Walker refers to in her essay and that Hurston depicts in *Their Eyes Were Watching God*.

Certainly in Celie, Walker selects an unlikely character in whom to explore the possibility of redemption. Like Janie, Celie is uneducated and psychologically abused. Unlike Janie, however, she is deprived and consistently physically abused as well. The character of Celie becomes, artistically, a supreme example of Walker's faith in human potential. Gloria Wade-Gayles observes that Celie's "psychological and physical abuse . . . lasts for decades. Celie's pain is profound and wrenching, and all of it is created by Black men. No pretty pictures of purple flowers growing in an open field and no emotional homecomings can redeem" her (50). Celie is raped by her mother's husband, taken out of school because she is pregnant, and deprived even of the two offspring of rape she is forced to bear; furthermore, she becomes sterile, and is married off to a widower who needs a hard worker to take care of him and his many children.

Yet, Celie's redemption in the classic rags to riches success story no longer seems remarkable or neoromantic when one examines Walker's statement that she is committed to exploring not only "the oppressions, the insanities, and the loyalties, but the triumphs of Black women as well" (O'Brien 192; Washington 133). Consequently, by exploring intrafamily relationships, Walker achieves redemption for a character like Celie, who represents the utter extreme of a hard-working, spiritless, and physically unattractive woman. For Walker, like Hurston, intrafamily relationships are one of the major concerns of her fiction: "All along I wanted to explore the relationship between parents and children, specifically between daughters and fathers and I wanted to learn myself, how it happens that the hatred a child can have for a parent becomes inflexible" (O'Brien 197).

Pa strikingly illustrates Walker's exploration of this concern, for Celie's story reveals a vivid picture of the physical and psychic abuse she and her mother suffer during his sexual onslaught. According to Celie's narrative, Pa barely waits for one child to be born, and more importantly for the mother to heal, before he is ready to start another. No one's tears or ills seem to matter in the face of Pa's lust. After her mother dies screaming and cussing, Celie writes that Pa comes home married to a girl Celie's age. Pa demands sex of the girl so often that she appears dazed, wooden, and walks around in a trance. In only a few pages, Walker illustrates in her depiction of three physically and psychologically abused women within the family unit a community of women whose potential for creativity may have been thwarted or stifled.

When Pa continues his promiscuity and lust, in spite of the presence of his new bride, Celie does what she can to protect her sister Nettie, offering herself as a "sacrifice" to Pa instead. Despite being torn by contrary instincts while suffering physical and psychological abuse, Celie creates her own idea of feminine beauty—horsehair, feathers, and high heel shoes—and her promiscuous and God-like father accepts the sacrifice offered him.

Because Celie bears the brunt of sexual and emotional abuse to spare her sister, it becomes imperative for her to write to God. In writing to Him, she settles into impenetrability, into a sanctuary from further pain. Out of the bits and pieces allowed her—Celie's thoughts as she writes to God—she creates a work of art, primitive though it be, in order to redeem herself. Even in marriage, Celie manifests her potential for creativity in figuratively becoming a tree. In order to survive and affirm her real self, Celie goes through a mock death. She becomes a fearful tree. Like Nanny and Janie, Celie fashions out of her personal thoughts a work of functional art in order to survive. Like Janie, she thinks creative thoughts in order to save herself.

Although Walker focuses on Celie in *The Color Purple*, most of the women in the novel are examples of women who are physically and psychologically abused and torn by contrary instincts: Sofia, Celie's daughter-in-law, imprisoned for sassing the mayor's wife; Shug, ostracized because she does not fit the conventional mode of behavior for a woman of her time—she smokes, drinks, curses, has given birth to three children out of wedlock, and wanders over the country singing blues. Nevertheless, these characters affirm Walker's conviction that the private and public world can be transformed. In this cruel and violent story of redemption, what matters to most of the women in Celie's world is giving the truth to those who need it, being freed from the suppression of one's will or talent, taking just what you need from people, and choosing for yourself. Like Pheoby in *Their Eyes Were Watching God*, they share, know, and assimilate each other's experiences. They become for each other models in behavior and growth of spirit that enrich and enlarge their own existence.

Walker explores redemption not only through incest, but also through another taboo and controversial life style in American society—lesbianism. As a writer, she admits that her actions mean "very often finding oneself considered unacceptable by masses of people who think the writer's obligation is not to explore or to challenge but to second the masses' motions, whatever they are" (O'Brien 204). One can almost visualize reading these words from the pen of Zora Neale Hurston, for she also explored issues and topics that were considered controversial during her time.

There is no doubt, however, that in dealing with taboo customs, such as incest, Walker definitely does not "second the masses' motions." Not only does she explore such controversial topics, she also uses them as redemptive forces, as a means of re-creation of the self. For example, the lesbian relationship between Celie and Shug, Mr. ___'s mistress, helps Celie to develop the capacity to nurture her own creativity through peacefully sewing and quilting. Shug becomes for her, as Celie had been for Nettie, a means of salvation when she promises not to leave the household until she knows Albert has stopped his physical abuse of Celie. A Christ figure for Celie, Shug raises her up from a mock death; in her encouragement of Celie's creativity, Shug offers her, for the very first time, a source of hope in her life.

The contact with Mr. ___ and his perception of her as family ultimately provide Celie a necessary context and a direction. Through them, she sees the way to continue the re-creation of her own self, her true identity. In order to go forward, Celie, like Janie, goes to the past. Celie's past in *The Color Purple* is of commanding and central interest when she confides in Shug the story of Pa's abuse, the selling of her children born out of the incestuous affair with Pa, and Nettie's departure to a place unknown. When the two women discover that Mr. ___ has been hiding for years Nettie's letters to her sister, Celie reacts by affirming her gladness in her ability to think and consequently to form thoughts that allow her to cope with devastating psychological abuse.

God, who has been present throughout the novel in Celie's writing to Him, begins to take on a new context and meaning for Celie when she discovers Nettie's whereabouts. Whereas Janie quietly accepts the circumstances surrounding Tea Cake's death as the will of God, Celie indicts God for his apparent nonchalance concerning her life, and ponders how an omniscient, loving God could let such suffering, abuse, and misrepresentation—obstacles to her redeemed self-identity—occur. In becoming her own person, she no longer writes to God. Instead, illustrating the network of female nurturance, as Janie does in *Their Eyes Were Watching God*, she writes to Nettie, using that act to dismiss her "God" of old, and embrace the more expansive and inclusive "God" of Shug's teachings.

By accepting Shug's explanation of the nature of God, Celie finally realizes that she must begin to embrace life in spite of her pain and sorrow. Moreover, she continues her potential for creative inspiration when she first designs and makes a pair of pants for Shug to wear on her singing tours. Soon Shug brings Celie so many orders that she has to hire additional help to sew while she devotes her time to designing. Reflecting the creative energy and love that go into each pair of pants, Celie names her new business Folkspants, Unlimited, a name that symbolizes Celie's entrance into the creative universe.

Through Celie, who re-creates herself from the fragments of human passions and neglect found in physical and psychological abuse, Walker depicts a confidence in the human spirit. Celie finds dignity through asserting her own personality and needs in designing fashion pants. Through her acknowledgment of God within, she further re-creates herself, seeing God as that "twin self who saved them from their abused consciousness and chronic physical loneliness, and that twin self is in all of us, waiting only to be summoned" (Steinem 89–90).

For the women characters in *The Color Purple*, as for Janie in *Their Eyes Were Watching God*, spiritual redemption evolves through the self. Thus, just as Hurston implies that Janie will continue a life of satisfaction following Tea Cake's death, Walker actually presents Celie accepting the physical absence of Shug in her life even as love continues. Clearly in this and other ways, Alice Walker adapts and builds upon the literary legacy Zora Neale Hurston established. *Their Eyes Were Watching God* and *The Color Purple* illustrate the similarities these two authors share in terms of their black female characterization and theme development. Surely, Walker's fictional emulation of character and theme acknowledges a greatly admired literary model, Zora Neale Hurston. Both authors vividly explore the Black female psyche in depicting self-recreation as effective revenge for pain.

WORKS CITED

Bethel, Lorraine. "This Infinity of Conscious Pain: Zora Neale Hurston and the Black Female Literary Tradition." In *But Some of Us Are Brave*, edited by Gloria T. Hull et al., 176–188. New York: Feminist Press, 1982.

Brown, Lloyd W. "Zora Neale Hurston and the Nature of Female Perception." *Obsidian* 4, no. 3 (1978): 39–45.

Gayle, Addison, Jr. *The Way of the New World.* New York: Doubleday, 1975.

Hurston, Zora Neale. *Their Eyes Were Watching God.* Philadelphia: J. B. Lippincott, 1937; Urbana: University of Illinois Press, 1978.

O'Brien, John, ed. *Interviews with Black Writers*. New York: Liveright, 1973.

Rosenblatt, Roger. *Black Fiction*. Cambridge, Mass.: Harvard University Press, 1974.

Royster, Beatrice Horn. "The Ironic Vision of Four Black Women Novelists: A Study of the Novels of Jessie Fauset, Nella Larsen, Zora Neale Hurston, and Ann Petry." Ph.D. diss., Emory University, 1975.

Steinem, Gloria. "Do You Know This Woman: She Knows You: A Profile of Alice Walker." Ms., 10 (June 1982): 35–37, 89–92.

Wade-Gayles, Gloria. "Anatomy of an Error: *The Color Purple* Controversy." *Catalyst*, premiere issue, 1986, 50–53.

Walker, Alice. *The Color Purple*. New York: Harcourt Brace Jovanovich, 1982.

——. "Saving the Life That Is Your Own: The Importance of Models in the Artist's Life." In *In Search of Our Mothers' Gardens: Womanist Prose*, 3–14. New York: Harcourt Brace Jovanovich, 1983.

Washington, Mary Helen. "An Essay on Alice Walker." In *Sturdy Black Bridges: Visions of Black Women in Literature*, edited by Roseann Bel, et al., 133–149. Garden City, N.Y.: Anchor Press/Doubleday, 1979.

8

Women and Words: Articulating the Self in *Their Eyes Were Watching God* and *The Color Purple*

Valerie Babb

When in *Their Eyes Were Watching God*, Zora Neale Hurston has Janie reflect on her upcoming union with Joe Starks that "old thoughts were going to come in handy now, but new words would have to be made and said to fit them" (54–55), the author indicates the importance of words in the formation of Janie's ideas and self. Alice Walker, seeing Zora and *Their Eyes* as supremely important, utilizes words in a similarly symbolic light in her novel *The Color Purple*.

Both Hurston and Walker use words to mirror the attempt of black women to find a voice capable of articulating black female identity. As such, Hurston and Walker are part of a larger group of black women writers who realize the importance of words to the black female identity. Perhaps Audre Lorde's eloquent description of the power of words and voice in her essay "My Words Will Be There" best illustrates the importance of words to the black woman writer:

> I looked around when I was a young woman and there was no one saying what I wanted and needed to hear. I felt totally alienated, disoriented, crazy. . . . I was very inarticulate. . . . I couldn't speak. I didn't speak . . . until I started reading and writing poetry. (Evans 261)

Just as a discovery of words releases Lorde's pent-up expression and allows her to discover a voice, so too will words allow Hurston and Walker's female characters to free themselves from an imposed silence and articulate their own identities.

While Hurston and Walker's use of words as symbols of self-knowledge is found in many literary works by black women, their common pattern of a character emerging from muteness to articulateness might derive from their similar experiences growing up in a rural southern environment, where, as Hurston states in her autobiography, *Dust Tracks on a Road*, the "average Southern child, white or Black is raised on simile and invective" (135–136). Whether taking the guise of the systematic insult game, the dozens, or the trading of tales, verbal acumen was often equated with personal power and worth.

In her autobiography, Hurston recalls an interchange between her parents in which her father expressed concern over her flippancy. As she recounts her mother's response, she indicates the importance of a fluent and assured use of language to the development of a strong female personality, and how that development is often thwarted by a male authority:

> My mother . . . conceded that I was impudent and given to talking back, but she didn't want to "squinch my spirit" too much for fear I would turn out to be a mealy-mouthed rag doll by the time I got grown. (21)

The significant implication of this quote and one that will evolve into a major theme in *Their Eyes* is that without "talk" or self-expression, a woman loses identity and independence.

In her collection of essays *In Search of Our Mothers' Gardens*, Alice Walker also stresses the importance of words in her life, acknowledging that she absorbed and passed on through her writings many of the stories, replete with appropriate cadence and mannerisms, she heard from her mother about her life. Walker's attitude toward stories, and by extension words, is again representative of one expressed by many black women writers. Toni Cade Bambara, for example, makes a similar statement in her essay "Salvation is the Issue": "Stories are important. They keep us alive. . . . Our lives preserved. How it was; how it be" (Evans 41). As it does for Bambara, so will the written word capture and preserve the oral tales that chronicle and interpret the experiences of Walker's black women.

Within both *Their Eyes Were Watching God* and *The Color Purple*, lexical mastery preserves experience and signals the growth of consciousness that results from such preservation. Hurston's entire novel might be said to represent Janie's searching for the words that will articulate her identity. Words within this book and several of Hurston's other works are more than just communicative devices; the ability to find and use them to create a language of self-definition symbolically indicates the degree of a character's self-knowledge and self-love.

Like Hurston, Walker too employs lexical imagery, but augments this imagery in *The Color Purple*. Where the words that would allow Hurston's characters to express their identities are oral ones, the words that would do the same for Walker's characters are written ones, as the epistolary form of her novel exemplifies. Through written expression, both Celie and Nettie are able to lend coherence to their transient world of sexual and emotional violation, gain a deeper understanding of themselves, and gain a greater awareness of their personal worth. For both authors, once women acquire lexical power, they create a self-derived definition of themselves that leads to greater control of their lives.

Whether in the form of "talk" or writing, Hurston and Walker are acutely aware of the importance of words in asserting independence, as well as in defining and preserving identity. In *Their Eyes* and *The Color Purple*, words enable each major female figure to transform her muted voice into one able to articulate distinctly who she is and the value of her experience.

The world in *Their Eyes* is one in which words confer humanity. "Tongueless, earless . . . conveniences" become "powerful and human" once "the sun and the bossman" are gone, because of the ability to use words to articulate their experiences. As the novel opens, the dwellers of the town are gathered, after a long workday, on a front porch along a major road waiting for the chance to talk, gossip—to use words and hence through their articulations to assert their independence and humanness:

> These sitters had been tongueless, earless, eyeless conveniences all day long. Mules and other brutes had occupied their skins. But now, the sun and the bossman were gone, so the skins felt powerful and human. They became lords of sounds and lesser things. They passed nations through their mouths. . . . A mood come alive. Words walking without masters. (10–11)

Hurston's analogy, which contrasts mules and brutes to "lords of sounds," links words to the freedom to become oneself and the power to create one's own reality. Hurston further develops the relationship between words and self-assertion as the novel continues. Each character's strength is defined in direct proportion to his or her verbal capability, and it is this capability that Janie, the novel's main character, must develop, if she is to develop at all.

When we first meet Janie, she is a child, nicknamed "Alphabet," because, as Janie states, "so many people had done named me different names" (21). The act of names being imposed upon her and the image of random letters of the alphabet waiting to be formed into words initially show Janie as an unfulfilled character seeking self-definition, rather than the definition given her by others. Hurston expresses Janie's lack of self-definition through a lack of verbal expression. Janie's yearning for a mode through which she can articulate the ideas pent up within her parallels her search for her identity. It will take a marriage to Logan Killicks, common-law marriages to Joe Starks and Vergible "Tea Cake" Woods, and Tea Cake's death for Janie to move from the randomness implied in her childhood nickname to the order that will result when she is able to find words and form self-articulatory statements from these words.

Janie's quest for independence is thwarted because she does not know that only she can articulate who she is; instead, she leaves this task to others. The first is her grandmother, Nanny, another black woman whose self-articulation has been stymied by being a woman and by being a slave. For Nanny, the black woman "is de mule uh de world" (29), and Nanny, too, seeks words to free her from a beast-of-burden status. She finds these words and uses them to define a vicarious identity through Janie. Rather than allow Janie the freedom to discover the words to create her own text and identity, Nanny wants to impose her words and text on Janie:

> Ah wanted to preach a great sermon about colored women sittin' on high, but they wasn't no pulpit for me. Freedom found me wid a baby daughter in mah arms, so Ah said Ah'd take a broom and cook-pot and throw up a highway through the wilderness for her. She would expound what Ah felt. But somehow she got lost offa de highway and next thing Ah knowed here you was in de world. So whilst Ah was tendin' you of nights Ah said Ah's save de text for you. (31–32)

To ensure that Janie has at least financial and social security, a marriage to Logan Killicks becomes an integral part of the text Nanny creates for her. But Janie's relationship with Logan deteriorates, and a discovery of words indicates the sense of self Janie gains as she constructs an identity that will not include Logan. As Janie contemplates her first self-actualizing step, leaving Logan, we see a volubility in Janie we have not seen before. Her first inklings of what she does not want for herself (if not yet, what she wants) dawn, and she articulates these feelings for Logan. It is interesting to note, that in direct proportion to the increase in Janie's power with words, Logan's power decreases. Trying to appear unaffected by Janie's question, "S'posin' Ah wuz to run off and leave yuh sometime," Logan feigns nonchalance and silences his true feelings:

> There! Janie had put words to his held-in fears. She might run off sure enough. The thought put a terrible ache in Logan's body, but he thought it best to put on scorn. (51)

Much of Logan's identity is derived from Janie's presence as his wife, and once this presence is gone, his loss of identity is reflected through loss of words.

As Janie continues her quest for self-definition, each major phase is indicated through a direct reference to words. In leaving Logan for Joe Starks, a man she thinks will be the "bee for her bloom" (54), Janie expresses optimism in an allusion to words:

> From now on until death she was going to have flower dust and springtime sprinkled over everything. . . . Her old thoughts were going to come in handy now, but new words would have to be made and said to fit them. (54–55)

Janie seeks new words to access the reservoir of thoughts within her and to enable her to form these thoughts into coherent self-expression.

Janie's relationship with Joe is not destined to fulfill her, and her sense of foreboding is also represented through words, as she realizes that "Joe didn't make many speeches with rhymes to her, but he bought her the best things" (56). While Joe can give Janie material comfort, he does not allow her to articulate herself; instead, he insists that she become his ornamental appendage and repress her self-expression:

> Time came when she fought back with her tongue as best she could, but it didn't do her any good. It just made Joe do more. He wanted her submission and he'd keep on fighting until he felt he had it. (111)

Joe makes several attempts to control Janie, and most are manifested through his desire to silence her and limit her access to words. He denies her the pleasure of contributing her anecdotes to the "lyin' " sessions on his porch, and denies her the opportunity to create stories about the town mule.

Like Logan, Joe feels a wife should be silent and submissive. When Janie is not malleable and attempts to speak for herself, Joe mutes her until Janie takes an assertive stand and publicly *speaks* her mind against him. During a fluent application of the dozens, Janie deftly uses words to emasculate Joe, and ironically, as Janie finds a new verbal expression, Joe is left a victim of a verbal attack and a man without words:

> Janie had . . . cast down his empty armor before men and they had laughed. . . . What can excuse a man in the eyes of other men for lack of strength? . . . The cruel deceit of Janie! Making all that show of humbleness and scorning him all the time! . . . Joe Starks didn't know the words for all this but he knew the feeling. So he struck Janie with all his might. (123–124)

As in the scene where Janie leaves Logan, Hurston simultaneously uses words to symbolize one character finding a voice and hence an identity, and another losing a voice and hence self-worth.

The emptiness in Janie's relationship with Joe is a result of their mutual inability to devise a communicative language. Unable to talk to Joe, Janie creates internal conversation, and in the stream of consciousness passages where Janie begins to analyze her relationship with Joe and the path of her life, we see a Janie more aware of herself. She realizes the impact each person involved in her life has had in shaping her, from Nanny, who "had twisted her so in the name of love" (138) to Joe, who "squeezed and crowded" her mind to make room for his in hers (133). She also realizes that she has let others define her, and that it is now time that she define herself. This realization culminates in Janie taking charge of words and molding them into a final speech to Joe on his deathbed in which she expresses all her dammed emotion and purges herself of inarticulated thought. From this point and for the rest of the novel, a more verbal Janie emerges with an increased self-awareness.

With a greater knowledge of herself, Janie is now ready to make her own decisions as to the course her life will take. This significant milestone is marked by the start of her relationship with Tea Cake, and an ability freely to use words. "Tea Cake wasn't strange. Seemed as if she had known him all her life. Look how she had been able to talk with him right off!" (151).

Tea Cake encourages Janie to break from the social constraints that artificially attempt to define what a woman should be and do, and instead develop her own identity. Through his taking her hunting, fishing, teaching her to drive, and asking her to work alongside him in the muck, Tea Cake allows Janie to develop her own definition of who she is, and with this definition comes a verbal freedom she has never known:

> Sometimes Janie would think of the old days in the big white house and the store and laugh to herself. What if Eatonville could see her now. . . . The men held big arguments here like they used to do on the store porch. Only here, she could listen and laugh and even talk some herself if she wanted to. (200)

The phrase "if she wanted to" indicates Janie's expressive freedom becoming synonymous with the freedom that comes from her entering the traditionally male domain of words, and using them to assert and define her own identity.

Throughout the novel, we see that Hurston equates a strong positive identity with a strong command of words. Words become a metaphor for self-definition: when Janie realizes her identity as an independent woman, it is represented through a new ability to articulate her thoughts; when Joe and Logan are stripped of their "illusion of irresistible maleness" (123), their dejection is represented through an inability to reply to Janie's verbal onslaught. Hurston's use of word imagery is key to understanding the psychological development of her characters, her female ones in particular. Hurston's cultural background and her understanding of the relatively mute position of black women in American society combined to influence her novel and give a unique perception of words and their power to aid in a black woman's self-definition.

The most significant indicator of Janie's arrival to selfhood and her ability to use language is the overall structure of the novel itself. *Their Eyes Were Watching God* is actually a flashback, a retelling of Janie's experiences to her friend Pheoby. Only after Janie has found her words, is comfortable with them, and truly knows they are hers, can she now tell her story, and only then can the flashback within the novel begin.

Like the structure of *Their Eyes*, the structure of *The Color Purple* also indicates the centrality of words to the novel's theme. The epistolary form of the work draws attention to the act of writing, and thus to words. Lexical potency is similarly integral to the development of the women in *The Color Purple*. Like Janie, Celie and Nettie will use the power of words to gain greater insights into their own natures and to make sense of their experiences as women. Again, we see here that a greater command of words usually indicates a greater knowledge of self and a greater command over one's life. Walker has taken Hurston's emphasis on the power of articulated or spoken words, and extended it to include the written word. Both sisters in *The Color Purple* speak through their writing, and they use the permanence of the written word to capture and analyze the events of their lives and their perceptions of themselves.

The world in which fourteen-year-old Celie finds herself is one in which she *must* use words, for she writes to understand. In her first letter to God, she asks Him to tell her why the man she believes is her father (but who is actually her stepfather) repeatedly rapes her, impregnates her twice, and takes from her the two children she has borne. Because her stepfather tells her that she had better not tell anyone about any of this, Celie, like Janie, is a woman silenced. Out of desperation, a muted Celie turns to the written word to alleviate her confusion, shame, and the silence that has been imposed upon her.

When Celie's stepfather marries her to Albert, a man who views her as a brute convenience, and when Albert forces the separation of Celie from her sister, Nettie, the only person she feels truly loves her, Celie continues to record her feelings in the form of letters to God. Several years later, with the aid of her female friend and subsequent lover, Shug Avery, Celie discovers Albert has kept Nettie's letters from her. The letters record Nettie's thoughts and experiences as she is separated from Celie, is employed by a missionary minister and his wife, and journeys to Africa with them as a missionary herself. Although the sisters lead very separate and different lives, words are important to each of them. The more Celie writes, the more she is able to analyze her experience and subsequently herself. Like Celie, Nettie, too, feels compelled to place her experience in words, so that she may gain a greater awareness of her consciousness.

Both Celie and Nettie instinctively sense that freedom from their oppressive world emerges from the word, and they also know words are the bond that will hold them together and fortify them against the dominance and abuse of a male world. Thus, as Nettie leaves Celie, she acknowledges that only death will keep her from writing to her sister. This linkage of life, death, and writing illustrates just how vital lexical access will be to the sisters' personal, psychological, and familial survival.

While words are certainly the bond joining the two sisters, they are also the vehicles that allow for the articulation of the self. Celie's entreaties to God in the opening paragraph of the novel show a confused character searching for herself and a sense of her place in the world. She asks God to explain to her why she, a fourteen-year-old who has always been a "good girl," must experience this "something" that she can neither articulate nor understand. Through using her words to write, Celie attempts to lend clarity to her experience by fixing it in a text that will aid in her introspection.

For Celie, words are the means that afford her deep self-examination. As she writes, she becomes more aware of herself, and this awareness, in turn, affects her writing, which becomes more artistically expressive. The more she knows who she is and values herself, the less her writing about her feelings consists of the mere statement of situational facts, and the more it consists of metaphors for her feelings, particularly nature metaphors, since nature, like Celie, has also been exploited by man. As she describes her pain and humiliation during the routine beatings administered by her husband, Albert, she makes an analogy between her experiences and nature's, choosing to make herself wood like a tree.

While Celie's writing documents her early experiences as Albert's wife, it also documents her poor self-esteem. When Nettie suggests that Celie stand up to Albert, Celie merely replies that she cannot, that she simply must obey her husband. We can note how her tone changes after she writes and views her experiences on paper, and after she receives the words Nettie has created for her. With a new self-esteem comes a new ability to use words even against Albert. In a sharp retort to Albert's delineating what he perceives are her faults, Celie's new confidence is evident: she explains that while she may be poor, black, and ugly, she is nonetheless here (187).

As was the case with Janie, once Celie discovers her own words and pairs them with those of Nettie, a stronger Celie emerges. During her final confrontation with Albert, we can note echoes of Hurston's technique in *Their Eyes*, where the image of words and loss of words indicate, respectively, one character whose self-image has been strengthened and one whose self-image has been threatened. While a now fluent and secure Celie can construct metaphors and similes to describe the situation, Albert sputters and is at a loss for words (see *The Color Purple* 181).

Through reading and using words, Celie is able to explore her own consciousness, assert herself against those who dominate her, and even question the nature of the God she initially wrote to for comfort in her life. In a very telling scene, Celie redirects her words from an old, white God who has been indifferent to her needs, to a new audience, her sister. No longer is Celie alone, thinking she is valueless, and writing only to a male God who does not heed her. She has found a real audience in her sister, and will develop a new, holistic interpretation of God, not as a man, but as a presence found in many things, including all of nature (164–168). In the salutation of her final letter, Celie is thus secure in her identity and is able to turn outward, see some of herself in all things, and address her observations and experiences to a universal audience that includes everything and everyone—all of creation.

It is important to note here just how Celie's heightened consciousness and self-awareness stem not only from her own lexical expression, but also from a coupling of this expression with the reading of Nettie's letters. Upon their discovery, and after Shug places the letters in chronological order for Celie, the shape and definition Celie seeks for her life begins to take form. In her letters, Nettie draws on their shared early experiences, adds them to her own in Africa, and formulates a new text for them both. Nettie uses words to strengthen the sisters' sense not only of who they are, but also of where they came from. By giving them knowledge of their African history, Nettie expands the self-defining use of words to include a cultural definition that complements the personal definition each sister finds through her writing.

Nettie begins her portion of the novel by relating the manner in which Albert attempts to thwart her communication with Celie. Here again, we see a woman who is silenced by a man in her life. When Albert accosts Nettie and she rebuffs him, he vows to take away words from both Celie and Nettie, promising that Nettie would never hear from Celie again. When Albert makes good on his promise and the silence between the sisters lengthens through the years, Nettie nonetheless maintains a mental linkage with Celie, acknowledging that in her mind she is always writing to Celie and imagining frequent responses from her sister. Obviously, that Nettie visualizes writing to Celie rather than just periodically thinking about her sister again shows how strong the power of words is, for they are the only instruments capable of bridging the vast distance and time gap between them.

In many instances, Nettie's use of words is similar to Celie's. Through them she creates a body of writing that can be viewed as a tool for introspection and as a private receptacle for thoughts and emotions too painful to be spoken. Not only does her writing nurture the articulation of the self, it also nurtures the articulation of a cultural identity and pride in the value of that cultural identity.

As Nettie learns more about Africa, she enshrines her discoveries in words to her sister. Step by step, through her letters Nettie creates a new world for Celie, and a new lexicon as she describes what she sees, equating the new thing with something with which Celie is already familiar. As she discovers the world of her ancestors, Nettie is able to take pride in her culture, and can now transfer some of this pride to her own self-image and Celie's.

Thus she records proudly the African past that had been severed from her own culture. She documents the village traditions, such as a welcoming ritual, and later the destruction of these traditions. Through recording the cultural wrongs committed by European cultures against Africans, Nettie is able to realize that her culture also has a history, albeit a history that is destroyed.

As much as documenting African traditions, Nettie's words also preserve the links that join African culture to African-American culture—for example, the interchange between Tashi, a child of the Olinka village, and Olivia, actually Celie's daughter, as they recall oral tales—thereby strengthening her and Celie's African-American identity. Nettie has thus used words and writing to investigate, record, and preserve cultural identity. In this instance, she has also encouraged her charges, members of a new generation, to do the same, thus ensuring, to some degree, the continuity of oral history.

In the experiences of both Celie and Nettie, then, we see the power of words to articulate and strengthen both personal and cultural identity. As Celie writes she establishes her own self-worth; as Nettie writes she preserves her cultural past and uses it as a source of pride as she forms her own self-image. For most of *The Color Purple* neither sister receives the other's letters. The capacity of words as communicative links is thus overshadowed by their capacity to aid in introspection and articulation of identity.

In Hurston, the power of the word is the power of the oral word as it is used to reflect a character's personal growth as she becomes able to articulate who she is. Walker builds on Hurston's symbolic use of the word, but for Walker, the word that is important is the written word. In both works, however, it is access to words that allows all of the women characters to find themselves and then place themselves in larger social and cultural contexts. It is not surprising that both these authors would focus on the importance of the word. Both Hurston and Walker are chroniclers of the African-American oral tradition, where words are existence. In their two novels, not only is the personal development of women illustrated through a growing facility with words, the importance of the word in African-American culture is also documented and memorialized.

WORKS CITED

Evans, Mari, ed. *Black Women Writers: Argument and Interviews*. London: Pluto Press, 1985.

Hurston, Zora Neale. *Dust Tracks on a Road: An Autobiography*. Philadelphia: J. B. Lippincott, 1942; Urbana: University of Illinois Press, 1971, 1984.

———. *Their Eyes Were Watching God*. Philadelphia: J. B. Lippincott, 1937; Urbana: University of Illinois Press, 1978.

Walker, Alice. *The Color Purple*. New York: Harcourt Brace Jovanovich, 1982.

———. *In Search of Our Mothers' Gardens: Womanist Prose*. New York: Harcourt Brace Jovanovich, 1983.

III

“The Humming”: Expanding the Connections to Other Works by Walker and Hurston

9

Searching for Zora in Alice's Garden: Rites of Passage in Hurston's *Their Eyes Were Watching God* and Walker's *The Third Life of Grange Copeland*

JoAnne Cornwell

> Kitty Brown is a well-known hoodoo doctor in New Orleans. . . . Her herb garden is pretty full and we often supplied other doctors with plants. Very few raise things since the supply houses carry about everything that is needed. But sometimes a thing is wanted fresh from the ground. That's where Kitty's garden comes in.
>
> —Zora Neale Hurston, *Mules and Men* (297)

Alice Walker keeps a garden, and from this space culls fresh inspiration for her art. Her garden is of the spirit, sown with seeds her poet's mind has gathered. These are seeds culled from life experienced by black women in America; the toil, the sorrow and joy, are gathered and planted in Alice's garden. These seeds from long ago and not so long ago sprout, bloom, and release their perfume through the pen of this most gifted fiction writer and poet. Walker's commitment to the resurrection of African-American creative expression through its women is well documented (see, for example, *In Search of Our Mothers' Gardens*). Her articles, lectures, and interviews reveal a clear sense of mission and the development of her career as a writer. Through her sense of mission, Walker actively fulfills the legacy of Zora Neale Hurston. A comparison of Hurston's *Their Eyes Were Watching God* and Walker's *The Third Life of Grange Copeland* demonstrates the ways in which this legacy springs forth.

To many, Hurston seems to be the most liberated of all African-American women writers. Heeding her mother's words, Zora "jumped at de sun." She reached for a career as a writer all the while refusing to reshape her flamboyant personality, a gift from her culture, to the contours that post-Reconstruction America required of black women. She was fiercely proud of her black culture, having grown up in a self-sufficient black town where celebration of that rich cultural heritage was an unconscious daily occurrence.

Alice Walker's identification with Zora Hurston, as we shall see, is much more than ideological. The progression apparent in Walker's three novels, for which we find the blueprint in *Grange Copeland*, testifies to Walker's acute sense of being rooted in a unique feminine artistic tradition of which Zora Hurston is probably the most important precursor.[1] Hurston's work as anthropologist, folklorist, and writer served to establish in a very concrete manner the framework for the literary tradition in which Alice Walker participates. Through Walker's work, then, we see the personal, cultural, and technical aspects of African-American creative expression becoming concretized.

Zora Neale Hurston is indeed the spiritual and cultural godmother of contemporary black women writers. Her work, technically speaking, is an anthropology of rural southern blacks. Trained as an anthropologist, she traveled alone through Florida, Louisiana, and Alabama collecting the folktales, songs, street cries, games, blues lyrics, folk sermons, rhymes, and hoodoo and conjure rituals that document the historical uniqueness and wealth of African-American culture. Hurston's anthropology, however, was a personal one, full of the poetry that was itself a reflection of the people she studied—her people. Not unlike Walker, Hurston's research was in a sense a study of her "self"—her past and present, her cultural personality and psychology, her role as a woman in a male-dominated society. The revelations of her research enhanced her personal creativity, and her first two novels were examples of anthropology put to prose. What is more, the second of these, *Their Eyes Were Watching God*, stands today as one of the most important pieces of fiction writing by a black woman.

In this novel Hurston succeeded in capturing an authentic pose of rural blacks in America that establishes the novel as a hallmark of its genre. She photographed a tradition sitting on its own back porch.[2] Without romanticizing poverty or explaining away the frustration and violence it breeds, without boasting of the congenial and loving nature of blacks, Hurston produced a work of cultural affirmation. Furthermore, through her sensitive portrayal of the heroine of the novel, Hurston constructed what was extraordinary for its time—a praise song to womankind.

Their Eyes Were Watching God makes tangible the Eatonville, Florida, that has come to symbolize rural southern black life in Hurston's work. Many of the characters and situations in the novel have antecedents in earlier works, reflecting the brand of fictional and historical tradition preserved by Hurston. "The Eatonville Anthology," published in *The*

Messenger in 1926, is a collection of fictionalized anecdotes transposed from Hurston's experiences in the town. This work was published ten years before her second novel. Already we see figures such as the mayor/store-keeper/postmaster, Joe "Jody" Clark, and his "soft looking" middle-aged wife. The characteristic passivity of the latter foreshadows those traits apparent in the heroine of *Their Eyes*. We also find Mrs. Roberts, the "pleading woman" who comes regularly to beg food of Clark, and we find Mr. Brazzle's lean, mean mule. We meet these characters again ten years later, somewhat transformed in the novel. They have by now become folk figures in Hurston's storytelling tradition. The mule, this time belonging to Matt Bonner, proves worthy of his reputation if only in the imaginations of those characters who are, like Hurston, spinners of yarns. Mrs. Roberts returns as Mrs. Robbins, her "pleading" ways fully intact. Clark becomes Starks, and his wife comes to us as Janie, the heroine of the novel.

The value of this work lies not solely in its literary success, but in the manner in which the author brings to light the artistic framework underlying its form of expression. *Their Eyes Were Watching God* is everything folklore is: explanatory, moralizing, eloquent, amusing; it is both a lie and God's truth told just right. Hurston is not interested in the type of objectivity that would have placed Eatonville in the larger context of pre–World War II America. She is obviously being very selective in the parameters she lays down as the setting for her novel. She is "lying"[3] in the best Eatonville tradition, embellishing through subtle re-creations the mythology of her people. Her prefeminist views on life and society weave their way comfortably, via characteristic imagery, into the fabric of the narrative. Hurston mythologizes a feminist perception of her culture, and in so doing, she renders this perception culturally valid.

It is possible, by capturing the central paradox of folk expression (i.e., lying and telling the truth), for modern literature to elevate itself to the level of myth. Myth functions as the means by which a given culture elucidates life's mysteries. Underlying this aetiological role, however, is invariably a psychological one. Myth communicates how people experience these mysteries, and in this way, it becomes both larger and smaller than life.

The mythic mode finds expression in Hurston's work through characteristic images and metaphors that seem to boil life experiences down to concentrated formulas. Literal meanings give way to the symbolic, and the success of discourse depends largely on the author's skill in drawing the reader into that "voluntary suspension of disbelief" so necessary to the experiencing of literary reality. The author further seeks to universalize the particular cultural experience. Hurston does this through the deliberate interplay of the characters of her novel, who are visibly cultural stereotypes, with the heroine, who displays archetypal qualities. As an archetype, Janie's personal development within the novel indicates the extent of her untapped potential. Hurston says of her, "She didn't read books so she didn't know that she was the world and the heavens boiled down to a drop" (*Their Eyes* 66).

The imagery of the novel indeed brings one around to a mind time when "God himself was on the ground and men could talk with him" (*Mules and Men* 5). Nature is not only filled with that same vital force that animates humans, it is equally as rambunctious. Each new day springs out from hiding on to the town of Eatonville: "Every morning the world flung itself over and exposed the town to the sun. . . . The sun from ambush was threatening the world with red daggers, but the shadows were gray and solid looking around the barn" (*Their Eyes* 29, 45).

Hurston further exploits the mythic mode through her use of time in the novel. Though a dominant linear progression prevails, we sense that time is nonetheless somewhat autonomous, almost tangible, self-motivating, and so has an undermining effect on the linearity of the novel. Time speaks, tells one things, and Janie learns that there are "years that ask questions and years that answer" (*Their Eyes* 21). Time can be touched, measured out like sugar or flour. Janie realizes this as she learns how to deal with the stifling relationship with her second husband. "She just measured out a little time for him and set it aside to wait" (67). Time can be arbitrary in the way it orders one's life. This constitutes a fortunate turn for Janie and at age forty, after two marriages, she discovers the joys of first love with Tea Cake, who very adeptly explains to her how this is possible: "God made it so you spent yo' ole age first wid somebody else, and saved up yo' young girl days to spend wid me" (149).

When God sends Death, with his huge "square toes," to take Tea Cake from Janie, she questions Him on this matter because He has apparently been known to play tricks on mortals before. Janie does not, however, implore God. She asks questions as if she has a right to know the answers. This is not arrogance, but an honest reflection of how the character perceives the world and her place in it. The heavens are laid out according to familiar dimensions—dimensions the eye can see and the hand can touch. The universe is alive and accessible to Hurston's characters, and the imagery of the novel reflects these mythic qualities. The forces of nature, God, death, are as so many spirits with whom the characters share their ontological space.

In fact, the very personal spirit-populated heavens have their earthly and psychic counterparts. Everyday occurrences, activities, and attitudes are invested with a life force, so that laughter is seen bursting out of eyes and leaking from the corners of mouths. Porches discuss and expand on the events of the day, and Janie studies about life by questioning its emissaries, as when she questions "lonesomeness" about her true feelings. The "space" within, the psyche, is but a scaled-down version of the universe. Here, the soul has its seasons and its storms. Janie's emotional and personal development is, in fact, couched in the metaphor of a pear tree waiting for its season to blossom. When the right bee comes along in the form of Tea Cake, Janie is plagued by storms of doubt, which quite naturally come to her in personified spirit form. "In the cool of the afternoon the fiend from hell specially sent to lovers arrived at Janie's ear. Doubt" (91).

It is not surprising that Hurston's inside view of Eatonville folk culture should reveal the psyche of her main character in such a unique way: It is quite literally a place the spirit can move around in. This, Janie does from time to time, and it is while "digging around inside of herself that [Janie] found that she had no interest in that seldom seen mother at all" (76). In a similar way she discovers that she does not love her second husband, Jody.

> Janie stood where he left her for unmeasured time and thought. She stood there until something fell off the shelf inside her. Then she went inside there to see what it was. It was her image of Jody tumbled down and shattered. But looking at it she saw that it never was the flesh and blood figure of her dreams. Just something she had grabbed up to drape her dreams over. (63)

This inner space is at times for Janie a place where the spirit could hide out, as when she attends her husband's funeral.

> Janie starched and ironed her face and came set in the funeral behind her veil. It was like a wall of stone and steel. The funeral was going on outside. . . . Inside the expensive black folds were resurrection and life. She did not reach outside for anything, nor did the things of death reach inside to disturb her calm. She sent her face to Joe's funeral, and herself went rollicking with the springtime across the world. (76)

Such remarkable imagery, while remaining consistent with the rest of the novel in its way of illustrating a style of living, gives some insight into how Hurston's female character deals with the oppressive side of her life. Her reactions call to mind those of Alice Walker's "suspended women" trapped by circumstances that stifled creativity and growth.

Long before Janie was conscious of herself as a person, she was locked into a set of relationships she felt powerless to change. When the self began to flower, it was quite naturally set out in the inner garden of her mind, the only space over which Janie had any control. This place of refuge for the spirit provided her with a mechanism for survival, but at the same time, there was a real danger of this inner space transforming itself into a prison. Janie averts this danger when she realizes through her relationship with Tea Cake that her spirit can find transcendence in a manner consistent with the mythic cultural models of fluidity between the metaphysical and material realms. She also discovers the liberating power of a symbolic return to the source of creative inspiration.

One cannot ignore the mandala symbolism implicit in the imagery of this novel. Hurston's configuration of the inner space signifies not only tranquility and refuge for the individual, but also the potential for wholeness that can be revealed through the character's own searching. This quest for the experience of wholeness is central in the heroine's development. Tea Cake, "a glance from God" (90), is the Apollo figure sent from the heavens to serve as guide through the final phases of Janie's quest. These phases display all of the necessary elements of an initiation rite: separation, transition, and incorporation (Stevens 93). It is ironic but mythologically significant that Janie must slay Tea Cake to save her own life. He cannot accompany her to the other side. The symbolic conquering of "otherness" represented in the rite of passage is a solitary journey that the neophyte must ultimately make alone.

This is to be the most painful lesson Janie will learn, and Hurston aptly refers to this mythic ordeal as "the meanest moment in eternity" (*Their Eyes* 152). Janie witnesses the last hours of Tea Cake's life when his body is no longer a fit dwelling for his spirit. However, this demise brings about the realization that there is no ironclad space where the spirit is protected from all dangers. The only protection is in the freedom of transcendence. Janie's life with Tea Cake has shown her to recognize the reality of this spiritual transcendence. The last lines of the novel confirm the life force that Janie derives from the ashes of Tea Cake's memory. By succeeding in opening herself up to life's horizons, she has bridged the barrier between the outer world and her space within, between past and future, between death and life, and her soul can now move about freely.

> Tea Cake came prancing around her where she was and the song of the sigh flew out of the window and lit in the top of the pine trees. . . .

> Of course he wasn't dead. He could never be dead until she herself had finished feeling and thinking. . . . Here was peace. She pulled in her horizon like a great fish-net. Pulled it in from around the waist of the world and draped it over her shoulder. So much of life in its meshes. She called her soul to come and see. (159)

Their Eyes Were Watching God, and more specifically the character of Janie Starks, demonstrates the depth of Zora Neale Hurston's insight into the southern black cultural personality and its implications for the female psyche. Alice Walker's fiction is constructed, both in the historical and psychological sense, upon this framework. The character mold of Janie Starks constitutes a theme from which Walker has developed dozens of variations.

In *The Third Life of Grange Copeland*, we find a setting that presupposes the cultural and ontological orientations laid down in Hurston's work. Walker's novel, however, provides us with a new perspective on this cultural experience through a more complex imaginative format. The novel is more clearly epic and episodic in its structure. The character of Grange Copeland is a compound character embodying both a cultural stereotype and the archetype that emerges from it. Finally, the several women characters offer a variety of angles through which to examine Walker's "womanist" perspective on her culture.

The evolutionary treatment from beginning to end of the novel is both enhanced and undermined by appropriate shifts in narrative emphasis. At first Grange's wife struggles to reveal herself to the reader through a male-dominated narrative; she is seen almost exclusively through the eyes of their son Brownfield. Later, Brownfield's wife makes a brief valiant effort at assertion over her husband, which is reflected in a shift in narrative focus. As she meets death, however, we see her through the eyes of her children as someone who has aged much faster than their father. Finally Ruth, Brownfield's third daughter, surfaces as the complex, troubled, and troubling end product of the novel's narrative configuration. Her symbolic roles as daughter, mother, and wife converge to challenge the dominant chronology of the novel.

Grange Copeland's life unfolds in three phases. The first phase, or life, is spent as a sharecropper in the South. Hopelessly indebted to his employer (master), Grange resorts to brutalizing his family as the only means he has of exercising control over his existence. The second life is spent in a northern city. After much ordeal, Grange returns to the South to begin his third life, which is centered on Ruth and his dedication to preparing her for the world that he has discovered. Fortunately, Walker does not stop here, but weaves into her plot a thread of mythic consciousness, which transforms her novel into a playground for the spirits of things. This is done in a manner consistent with the Hurston model. Ruth Copeland does not merely occupy Grange's interest during his third life, she *is* his third life. There is quite literally an essence symbolizing this progression that is sustained by the structure and characterization of the novel, and that manifests itself in Grange, Brownfield, and finally in Ruth.

The reader becomes aware of this "spirit" activity soon after being introduced to Brownfield. Never touched by his father, Brownfield grows up through years of empty days of waiting for his mother's evening return. The awful necessities of the sharecropper's existence take their toll on the Copelands, and as Brownfield witnesses the final disintegration of his parents' relationship, he does so through vacant eyes no longer capable of showing or seeing love. At this point, the reader can no longer dismiss the eerie perception that Walker has constructed a being devoid of a soul. Brownfield is in fact a body inhabited by the spirit of his absent father. As Grange Copeland's son, he is the continuation of Grange's misery—he *is* Grange's first life, and it is through Brownfield that the contours of Grange's youth are revealed.

Grange's desertion of his family permits Brownfield to set out in search of himself. Here Walker threatens to allow her character access to the privileged community of the initiated. Perhaps he will acquire a soul. It soon becomes evident, however, that Brownfield cannot lift his feet from the path forged by his father's footsteps. He ends up spending several years being kept by a woman whom he later discovers to be his father's former mistress. The degeneration of circumstances we come to associate with Brownfield's life remains consistent throughout the novel, notably as his marriage to Mem degenerates to its tragic but somehow logical end. He murders her to reestablish his sense of control over his own emptiness.

That which dooms Brownfield so desperately to emptiness is not simply his status as a southern black sharecropper. The imaginative format of the novel accords him a double function—while he embodies Grange's first life, he is also the symbol of the liminality and ordeal of Grange's second life, which is unfolding simultaneously to his own, but outside the narrative context of the novel. Through flashbacks later in the novel, the reader learns of the most significant aspects of Grange's second life. Most important, the sacrificial death of a young white woman frees Grange to return south and begin his third life with Ruth. It comes as no surprise, then, that at the end of the novel, Grange must slay Brownfield, a vestige of his first life and a symbol of his second, for the sake of his third, which has been invested in Ruth. This calls to mind the slaying of Tea Cake by Janie, who must continue her journey of self-discovery without him.

Clearly the three "lives" of Grange Copeland evoke in an original way the phases of the archetypal rite of passage. Separation from familiar surroundings takes the neophyte into a mythic space of potential transformation where the neophyte must submit to ordeals, learn life's secrets, and prove worthy to be reborn into the world, renewed, transformed, ready to repeat the cycle anew on a different plane. For Grange, this constitutes leaving his family and subjecting himself to the bleakness of the north in order to effect an enlightened return. Brownfield's journey is in a sense a parody of the archetypal model. He is the stereotyped image of his condition, unable to rise to a level that would allow his spirit (if he had one) to transcend its original state. Totally lacking innovation, Brownfield is doomed to a mindless repetition of inherited patterns of being. He cannot break the mold that formed him, and this ultimately leads to his demise. Ruth's journey takes her from her father's household into that of her grandfather, and her years-long apprenticeship with Grange teaches them both a great deal. Grange's death signals the end of this apprenticeship and Ruth's entry into a new phase of her life, which goes beyond the story's end.

In anticipating what shape this new phase will take, the reader must not assume that Ruth is merely the end product of her grandfather's spiritual voyage. Unlike Brownfield, she is not simply a repository for displaced sensibilities. She is living out a destiny that links her through circumstance and her own spirituality to that of her mother and grandmother. One is not surprised to find represented here Alice Walker's evolutionary model for her women characters. Grange's first wife and Ruth's mother were "suspended women," each in her own way having tried to create more space into which the next generation of women might move. In fact, Mem's death literally propels Ruth into Grange's arms and the male world they represent.

Ruth, then, is the embodiment of both male and female transcendence. Already in this first novel, Alice Walker underscores the importance of the androgynous experience in liberating the spirit. This motif comes through even more strongly in her two later novels *Meridian* and *The Color Purple*. Not surprisingly, the androgynous imperative was anticipated by Zora Hurston in *Their Eyes Were Watching God*. Janie Starks takes on ways of being that were viewed as mannish in the eyes of her town. Though the novel does not really resolve this question, one senses that the heroine is more whole for having explored the male side of her nature.

In the last phase of his life, Grange, too, experiences an androgynous reorientation. He loses interest in his second wife; being with Ruth, he has no need for a woman. He has become not only the father to Ruth that neither he nor Brownfield had ever been, but also the mother, guiding her steps from childhood to womanhood. There is, however, something incestuous about their relationship. They appear almost as lovers in the endless hours they spend enjoying each other's companionship. Their love is in fact primordial and leads Ruth to the discovery of truths unlearned, about her ancestral past and about her present, and in turn makes her mothering of Grange seem somehow natural. It is significant that these truths are communicated not through words, but are sensed at one point as she dances with Grange to the accompaniment of his own hoarse voice.

In a sense, Ruth is Grange's third "wife." In fact, the substitution of this term in the title gives an important insight into the significant role Ruth plays in the transformations of both man and woman in the novel. As a kind of "new woman," she affords Grange the opportunity of being the "new man": nurturing and protective, a spiritual companion, but no longer abusive because no longer deficient. His life has been a success and ironically, because of this success, he must finally succumb to the rush of the evolutionary progression he symbolizes.

Finally, Grange leaves a legacy for Ruth to carry on. This legacy is not unlike the one left for Alice Walker by Zora Neale Hurston. Significantly, the final movement of the novel is set in a metaphorical garden. Having built a wall around his property, Grange secures all matters in Ruth's name, then "plants" her there as he departs this life. Like her predecessors, historical and fictional, Ruth will grapple alone with life's yet unseen creative imperatives. To some degree, however, the severity of these imperatives will be attenuated by the simple fact that Ruth, like Walker, will know where lie her roots.

NOTES

1. See Alice Walker, "In Search of Our Mothers' Gardens," Ms. 2, no. 11 (May 1974): 64–105. Here Walker discusses her notion of "suspended women" and pays tribute to the early voices, such as that of Phyllis Wheatley, who kept alive the "notion of song."

2. The "back porch" phenomenon in Eatonville is given symbolic importance in Hurston's work. The porch is the arena for social and political and interpersonal interaction, for entertainment, relaxation, and the "lying" contest that Hurston dramatizes in her fiction.

3. The tradition of storytelling, or lying, for sport produced local champions, and standards that were to be maintained.

WORKS CITED

Hurston, Zora Neale. "The Eatonville Anthology." *Messenger* 8 (1926): 261–262.

——. *Mules and Men*. Philadelphia: J. B. Lippincott, 1935; Bloomington: Indiana University Press, 1963, 1978.

——. *Their Eyes Were Watching God*. Greenwich, Conn.: Fawcett Publications, 1967.

Stevens, Anthony. *Archetypes: A Natural History of the Self*. New York: William Morrow, 1982.

Walker, Alice. *In Search of Our Mothers' Gardens: Womanist Prose*. New York: Harcourt Brace Jovanovich, 1983.

——. *The Third Life of Grange Copeland*. New York: Harcourt, Brace, 1970.

10

Dynamics of Change: Men and Co-Feeling in the Fiction of Zora Neale Hurston and Alice Walker

Ann Folwell Stanford

> Honey, de white man is de ruler of everything as fur as Ah been able tuh find out. Maybe it's some place way off in de ocean where de black man is in power, but we don't know nothin' but what we see. So de white man throw down de load and tell de nigger man tuh pick it up. He pick it up because he have to, but he don't tote it. He hand it to his womenfolks. De nigger woman is de mule uh de world so fur as Ah can see.
>
> —Zora Neale Hurston, *Their Eyes Were Watching God* (29)

A major tenet in the work of Zora Neale Hurston and Alice Walker is that racism is not the last word in oppression, and that to look at racism to the exclusion of sexism is to miss at least half of the picture. Beneath black men with their burden stand black women, historically unseen and unheard, eclipsed by the pressing issue of race.

Both Hurston and Walker expose sexist ideology by posing an alternative to what critic Elizabeth A. Meese calls a "phallocentric structure of knowledge" (143) where men and male-defined processes of knowing and being occupy the position of privilege. Hurston attempts to engage and shift worldviews such as Nanny's by creating developmental patterns that gradually move her male characters toward alternative modes of being and knowing where human attachment and compassion are seen as powerful factors in moral development—a development that goes far in disrupting a system of oppression based on race, class, and gender. Rather than addressing only race (reversing the racist hierarchy and placing black men rather than white at the center of power), Hurston (and later, Walker) begins to dismantle the very foundations and assumptions upon which phallocentric notions of power rest (and are wrested). Hurston relocates that power in the margins, where a new perspective privileges compassion and human attachment over detachment and domination. Walker further transforms these patterns into an alternative definition of maleness itself.

While many feminist critics have justly celebrated Hurston's depictions of black women as whole people, her remarkable extension of what Alice Walker calls "racial health" to some of her *male* characters has not been as closely scrutinized. Nor have critics looked much at the connection between the literature of Hurston and Walker in light of the specific dynamics and patterns of male development that displace phallocentric power structures and replace them with a structure of power resting on the ability to form attachments and relationships of care.

The work of psychologist Carol Gilligan illuminates the patterns of moral development in Hurston's and Walker's male characters, showing that the impulse in Hurston's creation of John Pearson of *Jonah's Gourd Vine* and Moses of *Moses, Man of the Mountain* is extended and more fully realized in Walker's Grange Copeland (*The Third Life of Grange Copeland*) and Albert of *The Color Purple*.

In her work on women's development, Gilligan has called attention to the need for a double perspective from which to view moral development: a "justice orientation" and a "care orientation." Two moral imperatives learned in early childhood, fairness and availability to those in need, "define two lines of moral development, providing different standards for assessing moral judgments and moral behavior and pointing to changes in the understanding of what fairness means and what constitutes care" (Gilligan 6).

Gilligan argues that "the two orientations . . . not only entail different notions of 'morality' . . . but also different conceptions of the emotions and the relations of the emotions with morality" (13). For example, activities that are dismissed from a justice perspective (caring for a child, planting a garden, sewing a pair of pants) may be seen as "significant and even central" when viewed from a care perspective.

> Detachment which is highly valued as the mark of mature moral judgment in the justice framework becomes in the care framework a sign of moral danger—the loss of connection with others. (14)

Attachment, or significant connection with others, becomes a primary focus of moral development when approached from a care perspective. "Co-feeling," as Gilligan terms it, "depends on the ability to *participate* in another's feelings, signifying an attitude of engagement rather than an attitude of judgment or observation" (17). While the distance between self and other does not entirely close, the presence of co-feeling tends to blur those boundaries, creating an interconnection that de-privileges detachment, valuing the feelings of the other as much as one's own.

Not surprisingly, studies have suggested the existence of gender asymmetry in moral development, with a care focus appearing in data primarily collected from girls and women. While Gilligan is careful not to overgeneralize this asymmetry, she does suggest that "men and women may have a tendency to see from different standpoints, or . . . to lose sight of different perspectives":

> While it is true that either we are men or we are women and certain experiences may accrue readily to one or the other sex, it is also true that the capacity for love and the appreciation of justice is not limited to either sex. (39)

Using Gilligan's framework, we can distinguish between the justice (and more masculinized) perspective, as that which emphasizes detachment and observation, and a care perspective, which focuses on co-feeling. Although these perspectives tend to be gender-marked, they are not biologically determined or limited. For the purposes of this paper, co-feeling is discussed as a feminine perspective, one that Hurston and Walker inscribe in their male characters by way of development, in order to expose and rewrite the phallocentric notions of power and self-definition under which their characters labor.

Addison Gayle, Jr.'s, statement that Hurston's men are less interesting than her women, who "receive more multidimensional treatment" (Gayle 39), is true only when what we are looking for is multidimensional treatment. Her male characters, while not providing penetrating psychological studies, frequently function as commentaries on cultural norms and values, showing through their impulse toward co-feeling that the possibilities of self-realization are not limited to women, but that traditional phallocentric assumptions about what constitutes power and maleness can be disrupted, decentered, and transformed. Hurston cuts through the "race question" and probes instead the "human question," displacing white hegemony for the moment, replacing it with inquiries into processes of human transformation that ultimately lead to a disruption not only of white hegemony, but of the blight of phallocentrism that crosses cultural and racial lines.

Jonah's Gourd Vine, Hurston's most autobiographical novel, is the story of John Pearson, the poet-preacher who pulls himself out of poverty by way of his intelligence, charm, and gift for preaching. Leaving his home to work on Alf Pearson's farm, John is sent to school and soon falls in love with the young and bright Lucy Potts. They marry, but John's compulsive philandering begins to fragment his marriage, and indeed it becomes the undoing of his marriage, career, and entire sense of self.

Lucy continues to support and encourage John's preaching, as his oratorical skill increases. John eventually becomes a leader in a Baptist convention in central Florida, out-preaching all contenders to his position of power. But his professional success only seems to exacerbate his marital problems; John and Lucy become more and more antagonistic, and he even strikes her. Lucy soon sickens and dies—perhaps because of the conjurations of John's mistress, Hattie—releasing John (he thinks) from his guilt. John marries Hattie, to the dismay of his parish, while "tales of weakness, tales of vice [hang] about [his] graying head" (221).

This marriage is less satisfying than the first, and John's bitterness and self-pity grow as he blames the dead Lucy for the misery of his marriage to Hattie:

> "You, you!" he sobbed into the crook of his arm when he was alone, "you made me do it. And Ah ain't never goin' tuh git over it long ez Ah live." (228)

After John discovers Hattie's plots against him and finds the objects of conjure she has used against him—"weird objects in bottles, in red flannel, and in toadskin" (253)—he beats her severely and she sues him for divorce on the grounds of adultery.

After his divorce, John finds himself without friends, church, or money. At this point John begins to turn from focusing blame on Hattie to looking, if not *at*, at least *for* himself:

> He sought Lucy thru all struggles of sleep, mewing and crying like a lost child, but she was not. He was really searching for a lost self. (285)

John's "courage [is] broken" (285), and he, having been the master of language, the preacher who was "an inspired artist who consecrate[d] language" and spoke "as God creating the world" (Hemenway 193), learns painfully to be silent:

> John said nothing. His words had been very few since his divorce. He was going about learning old truths for himself as all men must, and the knowledge he got burnt his insides like acid. (267)

Although we have little insight into John's internal struggle—we never learn what those "old truths" are for him or exactly for what "lost self" he searches—we do see that he grieves as much for the loss of interconnection and attachment as for Lucy herself. In fact, the frequency and almost compulsive nature of his extramarital pursuits suggest John's inability to form co-feeling.

While John undoubtedly exploits and abuses women, especially Lucy, it is nevertheless important to see that he too is entrapped in a system that oppresses not only women, but men as well. Judith Newton and Deborah Rosenfelt make a helpful distinction:

> where much feminist criticism refers to men and male domination as if men really were the free agents proposed by bourgeois and patriarchal ideology, materialist feminist criticism stresses men's relative imprisonment in ideology. (xxvi)

This observation is especially true for black men, who live on the margins of white society. In the work of Hurston and Walker, however, white society itself tends to be marginalized, and the black patriarchy becomes the locus of transformation. This transformation is nothing short of a liberation from ideology that circumscribes maleness by devaluing traits that have been culturally labeled feminine—compassion and co-feeling from a care perspective.

In an interchange between John and four of his deacons, we can see just this ideology at work. Up until his marriage to Hattie, the community has kept a blind eye to John's womanizing, but now they have had enough. It is not because John has married Hattie only three months after Lucy's death, nor is it because John's extramarital affairs run counter to community standards of morality. Instead, the criticism focuses on Hattie's character:

> Dat strumpet ain't never done nothin' but run up and down de road from one sawmill camp tuh de other and from de looks of her, times was hard. She ain't never had nothin'—not eben doodly-squat, and when she gits uh chance tuh git holt uh sumpin de ole buzzard is gone on uh rampage. She ain't got dis parsonage and dem po' li'l' motherless chillun tuh study 'bout. (217)

Hattie is a "strumpet" and a "buzzard," who fails to fulfill her prescribed role as a mother and a pastor's wife. The deacons criticize John for his choice of a mate and for his failure to live up to their standards of manhood: "You done got trapped and you ain't got de guts tuh take uh rascal-beater and run her way from here" (218). According to them, John should beat Hattie into submission and get rid of her. John's lack of prudence in choosing someone who is a "buzzard," and his inability to control her, anger the deacons and the community they represent. Bringing into her novel the discourse that privileges pretense and domination to the exclusion of human attachment and love, Hurston exposes its ideology and poses an alternative to it.

When John travels to Plant City looking for work, he meets Sally Lovelace, a woman who feeds him, gives him a job, and provides him with emotional support. As the relationship develops in ways that resemble that of Janie Crawford and Tea Cake in *Their Eyes Were Watching God*, John begins to move toward a feminized perspective of co-feeling and attachment based on mutuality. In a telling passage, Hurston places John in the position of a girl. On his wedding night, John was "as shy as a girl—as Lucy had been" (297), radically reversing his previous role as town womanizer.

While John's character demonstrates Hurston's impulse to move her male characters toward co-feeling, it is only the promise of possibility. After a return to preaching, John once again succumbs to temptation, and dies in a freak accident on his way back to Sally, "just as he approaches his greatest self-awareness" (Hemenway 191). Much as the biblical Jonah's gourd vine was cut down in the night, John's moral transformation miscarries before its fulfillment, but we see in this novel the glimmer of what Alice Walker will pick up and develop further in her novels—the displacement of male consciousness from a detached perspective and the inability to form meaningful attachments, and its repositioning in a context of co-feeling and caring.

On the surface, very little of John Pearson's developmental process occurs in *Moses, Man of the Mountain*, a novel critic Robert Hemenway calls "Hurston's most ambitious book" (256). However, as Moses, a larger-than-life folk hero, works to free his people from an oppressive power structure, he too moves toward what could be described as co-feeling.

Blyden Jackson discusses Hurston's transformation of the biblical story of Moses, "happily transport[ing her] readers to a position from which every Jew in Goshen is converted into an American Negro and every Egyptian in Old Pharaoh's Egypt into a white in the America where Hurston's folk Negroes live" (*Moses* xv–xvi). Pharaoh's court cruelly dominates and misuses human resources, coldly detached from the needs of the Hebrew "other." Moses, a member of Pharaoh's court by adoption, repudiates his position of power in Pharaoh's court and chooses to side with his people, the oppressed Hebrews, because he feels compassion for their plight.

Loosely following the biblical account, Hurston's Moses leads his people from bondage and slavery into the land of Canaan, a land of new promise and freedom. As Moses moves away from phallocentric systems, he experiences "a new sympathy for the oppressed of all mankind" and loses his "taste for war" (92). Moses, the mighty man of the mountain, looks at the Canaan he will never enter, and having "given Israel back the notes to songs," realizes that "the words [must] be according to their own dreams" (346). Moses refuses the privilege of ruling his people in Canaan, seeing in conventional power structures a profound emptiness.

> And what could he do for Israel that he had not already done? Nothing but live in a palace and wear a crown. . . . He had known palaces and the shadows of crowns had fallen athwart his head. He recoiled inwardly and felt cold. (348)

Moses has gained an "inside vision" (347), one that moves him to embrace what Gilligan would call the care perspective. It is a vision that subverts and redefines power relations, where to lead means to set free, and in so doing, to fulfill the terms of compassion: to feel and to be.

Alice Walker brings Hurston's discourse of male moral development into her work, extending its implications and outcome in Grange Copeland and *The Color Purple*'s Albert. Inscribed in Grange and Albert's characters are imprints of John Pearson's self-understanding and acceptance of responsibility for the failure of his marriage, and Moses' repudiation of the Egyptian (or racist) power structure and its characteristic systems of oppression and devaluation of human life. Walker rounds out Hurston's initial impulses toward co-feeling in her own male characters, insisting on the political and social implications of personal development and transformation. While, as she reveals in *In Search of Our Mothers' Gardens* (330), Walker's role models fell short of offering her the alternative for which she was searching, such an alternative appears in her art as she probes the possibilities for self-definition and development in her male characters.

Gilligan provides insight into Walker's strategy:

> The concept of identity expands to include the experience of interconnection. The moral domain is similarly enlarged by the inclusion of responsibility and care in relationships. And the underlying epistemology correspondingly shifts from the Greek ideal of knowledge

> as a correspondence between mind and form to the Biblical conception of knowing as a process of human relationship. (173)

Creating a new way of being and knowing for her male characters by exposing the lack of power in a superficially powerful cultural role model (manhood as detachment and domination), Walker replaces that model with representations of nurture and care. In this context, "knowing" occurs by way of human relatedness, and power accrues from the knowing that comes through compassion.

Grange Copeland, a black tenant farmer in Georgia, embittered and worn down by the material and spiritual poverty in which he lives, survives a demeaning and racist culture by cultivating detachment and later, hatred. Grange, who feels extreme emotional and physical detachment from his son, cringing from even touching him with his hand, epitomizes both victim and victimizer as he becomes increasingly cruel to his wife, Margaret, eventually deserting her, prompting her to kill herself and her illegitimate child.

Moving to the north, Grange comes to believe his survival as a black man rests on his ability to hate whites and, if necessary, to kill them. Barbara Christian's assessment that "Grange Copeland first hates himself because he is powerless, as opposed to powerful, the definition of maleness for him" (460) points to the crux of the problem with which Grange must wrestle: as long as self-respect is contingent upon the removal of the oppressor, power remains elusive and externalized, located in the alien other rather than the self.

Walker insists upon wresting power from the structures of oppression, both reversing its hierarchical principles—from external to internal power—and reinstating a new definition wherein internal and external power support each other. For Walker, power is not an either/or dichotomy, but both/and. However, Walker insists upon establishing first things first: external power without a corresponding internal power eventually collapses upon itself.

While parenting his granddaughter Ruth, Grange comes to discover that love endangers pride while hate leads to shame. The necessity of caring for Ruth and his growing love for her catalyze Grange's self-understanding, providing the opportunity for him to redeem his past two lives by finding purpose in showering Ruth with love. Grange begins to learn, much like John Pearson, "old truths for himself," seeing clearly his responsibility for the failure of his marriage and for his wife Margaret's death. No longer is it enough to blame the white man. In taking responsibility for his own actions, Grange defuses the power of white racist social structures. Much as Celie in *The Color Purple* has to stop thinking about men before she can clearly see anything, Grange has to take his eyes off the oppressor and just love himself and Ruth in order to see "straight."

Walker's model of male power is based on self-love and compassion. It is a power that identifies most closely with the maternal gesture. Grange not only becomes Ruth's "mother," but by the end of the novel, after he has been shot, he mothers himself in an act exhibiting an almost primal self-love, rocking himself into death. As Grange rocks himself into death, the maternal gesture fuses with the paternal, the two becoming indistinguishable, characterized by self-love and profound compassion.

Walker continues the dynamic of change in *The Color Purple*'s Albert. Epitomizing cold detachment and cruelty in his relationship with his servant-wife, Celie, Albert, like Grange, moves toward co-feeling and a new definition of himself based on his ability to love. Also like Grange, Albert is a victim of a race/class system that precludes self-definition and distorts the notion of maleness. Partly as a response to his own radically circumscribed sense of self, Albert vents rage on those more vulnerable than he.

A widower with children, Albert "needs" a wife. He negotiates for Celie's sister Nettie, but settles for Celie when her father will not let Nettie go. The negotiations proceed much as horse-trading would: they discuss Celie's physical strength, her health, her teeth. Once married, Albert treats Celie no better than a slave, often beating and verbally abusing her. After repeated (and almost unbelievable) cruelty and abuse, Celie finally decides to leave Albert—rather than kill him—and live with his ex-lover Shug Avery. Before leaving him, however, Celie vents a curse that Elizabeth Meese says "womanizes" Albert, placing him "in her position," where "he becomes an ally (more like her) instead of an oppressor (other)" (Meese 126; see *The Color Purple* 176). Celie's private version of the biblical text "what ye reap, so shall ye sow," radically displaces power relations between herself and Albert. And when Celie actually leaves, she concretizes that displacement, marking the beginning of Albert's development of co-feeling.

In his loneliness, Albert later comes to Celie for companionship. She observes the "womanized" Albert as he learns how to cook, creating his own recipes to get the sick child Henrietta to eat yams, and as he begins to collect shells. In one conversation, Albert tells Celie she reminded him of a bird when she lived with him as his wife, revealing his (then) blindness and (now) insight. Albert now perceives his lack of caring, of putting Celie at ease, as the mark of a fool, which is a significant shift in his self-definition. Other shifts begin to manifest themselves in Albert. Lacking purpose or direction, he asks Celie to teach him to sew. Now the "natural" man, Albert rejoices in his new sense of fluidity in gender roles, paradoxically becoming more of a man (or hu/man) as he moves closer to the gender-marked "feminine" co-feeling and attachment. He understands Celie's loneliness and has learned how to see beyond his narrowly circumscribed world of self/male and participate in something of the feelings and experiences of the other/female.

Not being tied to what "man" looks like sets in motion for Albert the process of letting go of constricting notions of maleness. Elizabeth Meese points out that "Celie's freedom from Albert's domination is coupled with his own freedom from the sociosexual economy" (126). Like John Pearson, who experiences "girlish" feelings, and Moses, who repudiates a power based on oppression, Albert discovers a new self emerging from the rubble of "disrupted sexual opposition" (Meese 126).

Walker does not simply leave Albert the happy owner of a new lease on life, however. Albert must, like Grange, recognize the suffering he has caused, a suffering he comes to identify with phallocentric modes of domination. Albert tells Celie he has learned from painful experience something about love. The loss of Shug, his crumbling sense of himself as a "man," and an ensuing loneliness function gradually to awaken Albert to his complicity in a cruel and blind system of oppression.

When Celie admits to Albert that she had told Shug about the beatings, Walker draws directly on Hurston's text in Albert's reply: that if a mule could speak, it would tell people how it has been abused (229). The two texts form a dialogue in which Nanny's claim that black women are the mules of the world finds voice and corroboration in Albert, confirming the critique of male hegemony found in *Their Eyes Were Watching God.* Walker inscribes "feminine" discourse into Albert's discourse, thereby blurring the lines between self and other, between "masculine" and "feminine." In addition, she shifts the power relations implicit in Nanny's statement from a dichotomized victim/victimizer complex, and reinstates those relations in a dialogue of shared responsibility.

"Breaking Chains and Encouraging Life," the title of one of Walker's essays, serves well to illustrate the dynamic that resonates throughout her work and responds to Hurston's impulse to envision lives freed from culturally determined racial and sexual stereotypes. In dismantling phallocentric structures of power and inscribing "feminine" patterns of development in their male characters, both authors provide frameworks for a vision of social change that depends upon a care perspective and a privileging of co-feeling. Gilligan writes:

> As we have listened for centuries to the voices of man and the theories of development that their experience informs, so we have

> come more recently to notice not only the silence of women but the difficulty in hearing what they say when they speak. Yet in the different voice of women lies the truth of an ethic of care, the tie between relationship and responsibility, and the origins of aggression in the failure of connection. (Gilligan 173)

When Hurston and Walker write the voice of an "ethic of care" into their texts, they disrupt patriarchal assumptions and norms. Both writers seek not only to undo stereotypical notions of maleness, but to establish alternative patterns of development, patterns based on the premise that within the context of an ethic of care lies the *possibility* of alternative modes of knowing and being.

WORKS CITED

Christian, Barbara. "Alice Walker: The Black Woman Artist as Wayward." In *Black Women Writers (1950–1980): A Critical Evaluation*, edited by Mari Evans, 457–477. Garden City, N.Y.: Anchor Press/Doubleday, 1984.

Gayle, Addison, Jr. "The Outsider." In *Zora Neale Hurston*, Modern Critical Views, edited by Harold Bloom, 35–46. New York: Chelsea House, 1986.

Gilligan, Carol. *In Another Voice: Psychological Theory and Women's Development*. Cambridge, Mass.: Harvard University Press, 1982.

Gilligan, Carol, and Grant Wiggins. "The Origins of Morality in Early Childhood Relationships." Paper presented at the University of North Carolina at Chapel Hill, October 25, 1986.

Hemenway, Robert E. *Zora Neale Hurston: A Literary Biography*. Urbana: University of Illinois Press, 1977.

Hurston, Zora Neale. *Jonah's Gourd Vine*. Philadelphia: J. B. Lippincott, 1934, 1971.

———. *Moses, Man of the Mountain*. Philadelphia: J. B. Lippincott, 1939; Urbana: University of Illinois Press, 1984.

———. *Their Eyes Were Watching God*. Philadelphia: J. B. Lippincott, 1937; Urbana: University of Illinois Press, 1978.

Meese, Elizabeth A. *Crossing the Double Cross: The Practice of Feminist Criticism*. Chapel Hill: University of North Carolina Press, 1986.

Newton, Judith, and Deborah Rosenfelt, eds. *Feminist Criticism and Social Change: Sex, Class and Race in Literature and Culture*. New York: Methuen, 1985.

Tate, Claudia, ed. "Alice Walker." In *Black Women Writers at Work*, 175–187. New York: Continuum, 1984.

Walker, Alice. *The Color Purple*. New York: Harcourt Brace Jovanovich, 1982.

———. *In Search of Our Mothers' Gardens: Womanist Prose*. New York: Harcourt Brace Jovanovich, 1983.

———. *Meridian*. New York: Harcourt, Brace, 1976; New York: Pocket Books/Simon & Schuster, 1976.

———. *The Third Life of Grange Copeland*. New York: Harcourt, Brace, 1970.

11

Zora Neale Hurston and Alice Walker: A Transcendent Relationship—*Jonah's Gourd Vine* and *The Color Purple*

Ayana Karanja

In the last quarter of the twentieth century, Alice Walker's novels, more than any others, are compared to novels written by Zora Neale Hurston several decades ago. Hurston and Walker are African-American writers who have created a kind of epic that often feels hauntingly resonant to their readers. This feeling of resonance is no mere coincidence, for Hurston's and Walker's readers experience déjà vu primarily as a result of two factors that induce these writers' shared worldview, as lived out by their fictional characters. These two factors are spatiality,[1] in that both Hurston and Walker were born and spent their youth in states that border one another in the southeastern quadrant of the United States; and cultural diffusion.[2] Runaway slaves from Georgia frequently found refuge in Florida, and thus advanced cultural diffusion, or the admixing of neighboring slave cultures. Some significant outcomes of cultural diffusion are values assimilation between groups, which includes gender role definition, similarity in, and exchange of language systems, or related styles of verbal communication, and, thus, commonality of worldview.[3]

It is small wonder, then, that the shared worldview of Hurston and Walker is made visible in their novels, particularly in Hurston's *Jonah's Gourd Vine* and Alice Walker's *The Color Purple*. As *Jonah's Gourd Vine* and *The Color Purple* are read in the temporal context of the women's movement in late twentieth-century America, their similar use of themes and conditions is, perhaps, more vivid than might otherwise be the case at an earlier or later point in time.

In these two novels, countervailing or dual themes of *vulnerability* and *ancient African female power*[4] are bound up in the female protagonists' lives. Both Hurston's Lucy and Walker's Celie are vulnerable, naive child brides who suffer physical pain and mental anguish in their marital relationships. Yet these young girls, living in the rural South in the early years of this century, search for and locate in themselves a power through which they find validation, self-affirmation, and peace, one woman in life, and the other in the face of death. Lucy and Celie speak their life and reflect their community's disposition in a regional patois, which is neither a Bantu tongue,[5] nor prototypic standard English, but an admixture of African languages and English,[6] born of an antecedent southern slave culture.[7] (In both novels, for example, we see the use of the pronoun "us" as opposed to "we": for example, "us is goin'," versus "we is goin'.")

Hurston's and Walker's use of the oppositional themes, vulnerability and ancient African female power, are coexistent, centripetal forces in their female protagonists' lives. In general, vulnerability reflects a youthful, naive, and guileless female presence, a personality disinclined toward real evil, wickedness, or wrongdoing. Ancient African female power, here, carries with it both ancient and traditional African cultural signification—a magical energy or force that can be made manifest in women in various forms, and with a wide range of outcomes.

From ancient Africa to the New World the belief in female power, acquired through supernatural forces, is not uncommon.[8] Many culture groups around the world believe that women can perform extraordinary feats, such as healing the human body, changing the physical properties of plants and animals, presaging events, causing abrupt changes in weather conditions, evoking a plague or drought, causing death without obvious injury to the victim, or concocting potions that will either kill or cure the same individual. Such women, it is thought, can draw lovers together or cause their separation, without direct contact with those affected. A "woman in her power" can induce male impotence or virility, barrenness or fertility in women; such a woman may have the power to cast spells of any duration, and can transform herself into nonhuman forms. Acts such as these are both explicit and implicit in *Jonah's Gourd Vine* and in *The Color Purple*.

Ancient African historical and mythological precedents exist for such female power, and are well documented in the form of female worship, handed down from generation to generation. The most powerful and widely worshipped female deities in African antiquity are the Egyptian goddesses Hathor, Isis, and Nut.[9] These goddesses' manifestations, or appearances, are interchangeable. For example, each of them appears from time to time in literature on ancient Egypt as the Goddess of Fertility, the Sacred Cow Goddess, the Self-Begetting Goddess, the Sky Goddess, and the Lady of the Sycamore Tree.

In more traditional and contemporary African life and history one might explore the influence of ancient goddess worship and female power within the context of Yoruba culture, in southwestern Nigeria, and in some areas in North and South America.[10] Among the Yoruba in Nigeria, female ancestors, or spirits, are known as the "Great Mothers,"[11] and it is believed that these women "own the world and everything in it."[12] These spirit women are invested with a supernatural power, or *ashe*, unrivaled in the Yoruba pantheon of spirits, goddesses, and ancestors.[13] The Great Mothers' power is obvious at the annual Gelede Festival in Yorubaland, when they are entreated through praise songs, dances, and recitations to come forth as their people, ritualistically, appeal to them.[14] They are placated and honored as a means of engaging their protection of the village community from calamity and misfortune. To anger or displease the Great Mothers is to court their wrath, leaving the community open to circumstance, if not evil.

The Yoruba give great care to ritual performance and to the wearing of appropriate masks and costumes during Gelede. Music, ritual drumming, utterances, and sacred incantations are practiced by performers, over and over again, for an error in presentation before the Mothers, "owners of the birds," might provoke their malevolent, as opposed to their protective, power.[15] Not unlike many other Bantu-speaking peoples, and their descendants, the concept of duality—good/evil, plentitude/deprivation, violence/peace—is at the center of Yoruba philosophy and worldview. Central to much West African thought, a Yoruba-like worldview crossed the Atlantic, unidentified and undetected within the slave cargoes, and, thus, was carried and diffused throughout the New World diaspora.[16]

Hurston and Walker have imbued their central female characters with great power, and that potential power, then, is in keeping with historical record and African tradition. Emergent from these writers' worldview are African-American icons and images of women whose lives unfold from their historical memory,[17] figurative agility, and first-hand knowledge of the rural southern woman's way with words. When shaped and ordered, as in the novels of Hurston and Walker, the southern woman's words are empowering utterances that reveal an authority oppositional to a life that may, at first, evidence only helplessness and vulnerability.

As daughters of the rural, African-American South, Hurston and Walker were steeped in the culture, mythology, lore, and oral tradition of their environment, one in which powerful female spirits, deities, goddesses, and gods have historical precedent, and their drama, both real and imagined, was transferred back and forth across state borderlines (Donnan 244). Florida, Hurston's natal state, was a haven for runaway slaves out of Walker's home state, Georgia. Thus, out of these particular circumstances, which include storytelling, oral history, and other lore, handed down across generations, these novelists build their female protagonists' lives.

In Hurston's *Jonah's Gourd Vine*, the life of Lucy Potts, a vulnerable fifteen-year-old girl, is seen through a prism of social dynamics that foreshorten her youth and render her a victim; ultimately, however, Lucy becomes a woman of vision and power. Lucy's mother, Emmeline Potts, promises her daughter's hand in marriage to a man many years her senior. Lucy, on the other hand, is deeply interested in marrying a young, poor man from the other side of the tracks, John Pearson (actually named "Two-Eyed-John"), a sixteen-year-old who was forced by his stepfather's cruelty to leave home prematurely. Uninterested in her daughter's romantic inclinations, Emmeline Potts declares:

> Here Artie Mimms is wid sixty acres under plow and two mules and done ast me fuh yuh ever since yuh wuz ten years ole and Ah done tole 'im he could have yuh, and here you is jumpin' up, goin' over mah head and marryin' uh nigger dat ain't got a changin' clothes. (127)

Her mother's disapproval notwithstanding, Lucy continues to see John, and their young love blossoms. Lucy shows John that she is charming and bright, as she recites her verses at church with correctness and conviction.

Persistent, John often accompanies Lucy home from church, despite Emmeline's objection. Emmeline, who is always strategically positioned to prevent any physical contact between the two, insists that John and Lucy always sit five feet apart, and walk with an arm's length between them. Lucy's father, Richard, on the other hand, is less critical of John's interest in his daughter, often verbally reprimanding his wife for her intrusions into the affairs of the young.

Hurston evidences her skill as a folklorist and her knowledge of African-American oral tradition growing out of the Old South as she involves John and Lucy, away from Emmeline's reproachful eye, in a standard southern courting ritual:[18]

> "Lucy, something been goin' on inside uh me uh long time."
> Diffidently, "Whut, John?"
> "Ah don't know, Lucy, but it boils up lak syrup in de summer time."
> "Maybe you needs some sassafras root tuh thin yo' blood out."
> "Naw, Lucy, Ah don't need no sassafras tea. You know whuss de matter wid me—but ack lak you dumb tuh de fack." (124)

Finally, Emmeline's objections fall away; young love prevails and is consummated in Lucy's marriage to John. As wife of John Pearson, who quickly becomes a minister, the vulnerable Lucy will soon be faced with the pain of her husband's extramarital affairs, and a strange alteration in his general behavior toward her.

Always considered a handsome young man, John is the target, and Lucy the envy, of many women in the Zion Hope Baptist Church, which John now pastors. A certain woman, Hattie Tyson, more than any other, is determined to drive a wedge between John and Lucy. The mediator Tyson uses is the local conjure woman—An' Dangie DeWoe—who knows the secret ways of invoking supernatural female power. This local female repository of magic power will place John under Hattie's influence and control.

Using explicit and implicit verbal symbols and signs associated with conjuring, Hattie and An' Dangie conspire to bring John under their power.

> An' Dangie DeWoe's hut squatted low and peered at the road. . . . The little rag-stuffed windows hindered the light and the walls were blackened with ancient smoke. . . .
>
> Hattie . . . said, "He ain't been."
>
> "He will. Sich things ez dat takes time. Did yuh feed 'im lak Ah tole yuh?"
>
> "Ain't laid eyes on 'im in seben weeks. . . . "
>
> She fumbled with the screwtop of a fruit jar and returned with a light handful of wish beans. "Stan over de gate whar he sleeps and eat dese beans and drop de hulls 'round yo' feet. Ah'll do de rest." . . .
>
> "G'wan do lak Ah tell yuh. Ah'm gwine hold de bitter bone in mah mouf so's you kin walk out de sight uh men. . . . Tain't nothin' built up dat Ah can't tear down."
>
> "Ah know you got the power. . . . "
>
> "Member now, you done started dis and it's got tuh be kep' up do hit'll turn back on yuh. . . . "
>
> The door slammed and An' Dangie crept to her altar . . . and began to dress candles with war water. When the altar had been set, she dressed the coffin in red, lit the inverted candles on the altar, saying as she did so, "Now fight! Fight and fuss 'til you part." When all was done she rubbed her hands and forehead with war powder, put the cat bone in her mouth, and laid herself down in the red coffin facing the altar and went into the spirit. (199–201)

Vulnerable and unknowing, Lucy and John now appear to be in the hands of female power, in the form of sorcery. Despite John's ministry, he, too, is without recourse in the midst of this scheme.

The Pearsons' marriage becomes increasingly difficult, and John is away from home for extended periods of time. Lucy, whose faith in John and their marriage continues, supports and advises John as he meets various attempts at the church to unseat him because of his reputation for womanizing. And, in spite of their marital problems, Lucy has borne three children.

By creating a minister in John, Hurston brings into full light the cultural linkage between African traditional religion and contemporary African-American religious practices. This linkage includes long, eloquent sermons like those preached by John at Zion Hope. Hurston clearly points out the synthesis of African and African-American religious practices: "John . . . never made a balk at a prayer. Some new figure, some new praise-giving name for God every time he knelt in church. He rolled his African drum up to the altar, and called his Congo Gods by Christian names" (145–146). Indeed, in a later work, *Moses, Man of the Mountain*, Hurston more definitively structures an entire novel around the life of Moses as an African figure, with unique spiritual power.

At the birth of Lucy's fourth child—her first female—we witness the exercise of ancient African female power, as used in relation to the management of the birthing process. Three women, one of whom is the community matriarch[19]—as distinguished from the sorcerer, An' Dangie DeWoe—are present. The community matriarch is familiar with the various rituals that accompany certain events, or rites of passage, in the community, and thus obeys or acknowledges their meaning. As an elder in the community, An' Pheemy, with two other women assistants, Edy and Della, aids Lucy in the birthing process:

> Pheemy with the help of Old Edy and Della performed the ancient rites. Edy and Della sweetened the mother[20] . . . but only Pheemy could handle the afterbirth in the proper way, so that no harm could come to Lucy. That is, she buried it shoulder deep to the east of the house, beneath a tree. (151)

The first daughter is named for Lucy's mother, Emmeline. Lucy's last child, also female, is named Isis, which is, as earlier noted, the name of the most powerful of all goddesses in the annals of history. This Egyptian goddess often appears in the literature as a sycamore tree. We might extrapolate that An' Pheemy buried the afterbirth under a tree, and, hence, under the protective care of a female spirit.[21] Here, Hurston also shows the dual nature of female power: An' Dangie DeWoe exercises her power for negative purposes—that is, driving the Reverend John Pearson into an illicit affair with Hattie Tyson—and, in contradistinction, An' Pheemy uses her special knowledge to perform rites and rituals of protection for Lucy during her vulnerable state following childbirth. One can also notice here the similarity between the precision in recitations, incantations, and the like, observed in Yoruba Gelede performers, and the restrictions of ritual behavior in a rural southern community, such as that only a predesignated woman may handle the afterbirth following the delivery of a child.

By the time Isis is a young girl, John's cruelty toward his wife is abundant, and Lucy is ill and in bed, obviously a victim of tuberculosis, aggravated by the psychological turmoil she suffers because of her mysteriously failing marriage. She asks John to come home evenings to care for their children, and John is angered by Lucy's insistence. Slapping Lucy's face on one occasion, John admonishes her, "Ah tole yuh tuh hush" (205). When John leaves the house, the child, Isis, brings Lucy's dinner, which she refuses. Preoccupied, Lucy at first lies quietly, and then tells Isis that she is "watchin' a great big old spider. . . . Up dere on de wall next tuh de celin'. Look lak he done took up uh stand" (205).[22] Isis offers to kill the spider with the broom, but Lucy declares, "De one dat put 'im dere will move 'im in his own time."

Lucy recognizes that her death is imminent. She calls Isis to her bedside, and explains her desire for Isis to have her feather bed, and emphasizes that the bed was her own, earned by sewing for a white woman. This is a statement with deeper meaning, symbolically suggesting that Isis should build on the foundation of knowledge Lucy has provided. She further instructs Isis to pursue whatever education that might be available to her so that she "kin keep out from under people's feet" (206). Lucy obviously believes that for women, knowledge empowers.

Lucy's next request of Isis is that she get the Bible and turn to the twenty-sixth chapter of Acts, where Paul's conversion experience is recounted. Paul, who is both a lawyer and a rabbi, has played a major role in the persecution of members of God's church, and he retells this conversion experience, which occurred on the road to Damascus. According to Acts 26, Paul saw a light from heaven, "about the brightness of the sun." The power of this light knocked Paul, and his fellow travelers, to the ground. Paul was blinded, but the others were not. While still lying on the ground, Paul heard a voice: "Why persecutest thou me?" And Paul asked, "Who art thou, Lord?" And He said, "I am Jesus whom thou persecutest." By alluding to this biblical passage, Hurston subtly foreshadows John's late awakening from the trancelike state through which he has functioned—often cruelly—while under the influence of An' Dangie DeWoe's supernatural power.[23]

On the morning following Lucy's talk with the young Isis, her neighbor and friend, Sister Clarke, questions her about the status of her relationship with God, to which Lucy responds:

> Don't worry 'bout me Sister Clarke. Ah done been in sorrow's kitchen and Ah done licked out all de pots. Ah done died in grief, and been buried in de bitter waters and done rose again from de dead. . . . Nothin kin touch my soul no mo'. It was hard to loose de string-holt on mah lil' chillun'. . . . but Ah reckon Ah done dat too. (209)

Sister Clarke, satisfied, urges Lucy, "Put whip tuh yo' hawses, honey. Whip 'em up."

Not only do we find that Lucy is at peace with her impending death, but she has given John a look—a gaze—on the night of their last encounter; Lucy's gaze conveys a forceful message to John, "stepped across the ordinary boundaries of life" (208). From that night forward, John greatly fears this physically vulnerable woman, and will not approach her bedside. Hurston has moved Lucy out of the realm of life in the world of the living and into a power that transcends earthly existence—into the power of the spirit world.[24] Thus, at the point of Lucy's greatest physical vulnerability, Hurston infuses her with supernatural power unprecedented in her life with John. The force transmitted through Lucy's gaze causes John to tremble, and he is afraid.

In Alice Walker's novel *The Color Purple*, we also meet a young, vulnerable protagonist, Celie, whom Walker locates in a rural, southern African-American community. Over the period of several decades, largely through letters written first to God, and later to her sister, Nettie, Celie metamorphoses into a strong, prophetic, and self-affirmed woman.

Celie's sojourn on the path to womanhood begins with the tragedy of multiple rape, which twice results in impregnation by her stepfather, beginning when she is fourteen years old. The stepfather, thought at that time to be her biological parent, is referred to as "Pa." Celie's mother, who is ill at the opening of the novel, dies. Celie is soon bartered away, along with her cow, to Pa's male friend, whom Celie calls Mr. ___, a man who is seeking a surrogate mother to care for his four children. (Their mother has been killed by her lover, and dies in the arms of her oldest son.)

The Celie/Mr. __ arrangement is double-edged, for it not only places Celie in a continuing position of vulnerability, it also leaves her younger sister, Nettie, with the stepfather and renders her more defenseless against his lust. Nettie rejects the stepfather and manages to run away to Celie, now Mr. __'s wife. In this new setting, once again, Nettie becomes the object of an older man's desire. Indeed, Nettie was the real object of Mr. __'s negotiations with the stepfather, who was unwilling to part with Nettie, but, instead, bargained Celie away, with her cow thrown in to make the deal more attractive.

At this point, then, both Celie and Nettie are kept busy outsmarting Mr. __ as he attempts to manipulate Nettie to his advantage. When Mr. __ uses sweet words and praises Nettie in various ways—her hair is beautiful, her teeth are white, her dress pretty—she ignores these fanciful lures, and passes his commentary on to Celie, who was called ugly by their stepfather. Over time, Celie begins to internalize many of Nettie's thrown-away compliments from Mr. __, and starts to see herself as pretty (18).

Through Mr. __'s son, Harpo, Walker introduces Sofia, a strong-looking young woman, who is pregnant, and who becomes Celie's stepdaughter-in-law. The ancient meaning of the name Sofia is "pure feminine spirit . . . a spiritual whole."[25] Sofia appears to be the antithesis of female vulnerability; she is a free-spirited young woman who is incredulous at the absence of self-will in Celie. Walker depicts Sofia as a woman who creates a scene whenever and wherever she believes her right to freedom is being jeopardized. Sofia tells Celie that she has always had to fight for her freedom—fight her brothers, her uncles, and now Harpo, her husband. Both Harpo and Celie are confounded by Sofia's strong will. For example, at the time of Sofia's mother's death, she and her "Amazon sisters" plan to be pallbearers at their mother's funeral. Walker's use of the term Amazon to describe Sofia and her sisters calls to mind the ancient Dahomyean Amazons, the great archers, who, as children, had their right breast seared off to enhance their accuracy in battle (Kanter 93).

Because Sofia is so strong-willed and Harpo is in shock, they fight often, in scenes described graphically in the novel (see, for example, *Color Purple* 36). Celie actually causes one of Harpo's and Sofia's battles. Since Harpo is baffled by the perfect control his father exerts over Celie, he feels less than a man because of his inability to control Sofia. In desperation he asks Celie how he can force Sofia to mind him the way she minds Mr. __. Grudgingly, Celie suggests that he beat Sofia, which, of course, is a useless effort. For his trouble, Harpo wears a black eye and many bruises. Celie has guilt. Sofia, of course, prevails.

Sofia, the warrior woman, ultimately suffers the consequences of a woman out of her place in society. Harpo and Sofia part, and each of them initiates a relationship with someone new. It is Sofia who leaves home, and takes up an affair with a man Walker calls a prizefighter, but who is more commonly known as Buster.

One afternoon Sofia and Buster take her six children to town, and the white mayor and his wife, Miss Millie, stop so that the wife can touch and admire Sofia's children for their cleanliness. Miss Millie finally asks Sofia to be her maid. Sofia staunchly refuses. Outraged and insulted, the mayor slaps Sofia, and Sofia, not the prizefighter, flattens him. For this breach of proper behavior, Sofia, the Amazon, is given a twelve-year prison sentence and an awesome, mutilating beating at the town jail. At the end of eleven and a half years, Sofia receives six months off for good behavior, and a job working for the mayor's wife, by day. At night she is forced to sleep under the mayor's house, on the ground. Over the course of Sofia's prison sentence, her children have grown up and no longer recognize her. Thus, Walker makes it clear that a woman's outward expression of dignity and self-affirmation can be extremely dangerous in many ways. And, through the juxtaposition of Celie and Sofia, she clearly illustrates oppositional or dual character types.

Walker moves Celie across time and space from vulnerability to full womanhood through three specific events or stages. Because of the dramatic and rhythmic change that occurs in Celie during each of these stages, the whole of her experience becomes a ritual of transformation. Celie's maturation process, therefore, is a rite of passage as delineated by Arnold Van Gennep's theory and configuration of the ritual process. Van Gennep describes three specific ritual phases—*separation*, *initiation*, and *incorporation*. According to Van Gennep, all celebratory transitions that occur with individuals or groups can be analyzed or understood through this model.[26]

Celie's first ritual stage is two-dimensional, and is marked by the death of her mother and separation from her community of orientation—most dramatically from her sister, Nettie. After Nettie runs away from Pa, and joins Celie in Mr. __'s houschold, she is, again, a potential rape victim, who is, ultimately, ejected from her new home because she and Celie have successfully guarded against Mr. __'s attempts to lure and catch Nettie. Celie gives Nettie the only thing she has that might be helpful—the name of a minister whose wife she met at the dry goods store in town. The woman had a little girl with her whom Celie believed to be her own daughter, Olivia, an infant gotten rid of by Pa shortly after her birth. Celie had questioned the woman in some depth about the child, but had no certainty, although her heart told her the child was hers (see *Color Purple* 14). Nettie leaves, locates the family, and becomes governess for their two children.

Celie's second ritual stage, initiation, is, by far, the longest and most difficult, though not unusual for rites of passage. In many world cultures, rites of initiation are symbolic of one's maturity or readiness to assume the circumscribed responsibilities of that society. Often the ceremonies associated with initiation require some physical change in the initiate, such as scarification, head-shaving, blood-letting, or a combination of these and other outward signs and symbols of inner change or transformation. Also, along with the physical marking, there may well be recitation of memorized ritual, sacred words, or incantations. Celie's initiation is represented through a number of events, her relationship with Shug Avery being the most evolutionary and meaningful.

Shug Avery has been Mr. __'s not-so-secret lover for many years; he is the father of her three children, children born while Mr. __ was still married to his first wife, Annie Julia. When Celie learns that Shug Avery is coming to Mr. __'s house, she becomes excited. To Celie, Shug Avery is a combination mystery woman and movie star. Shug's picture is the first one of a real person Celie has ever seen. On the other side, there is Mr. __'s father, who considers his son's relationship with Shug the worst possible fate that could befall his son. For him, Shug Avery is simply Mr. __'s whore. Shug is seen, by still others, as a good blues singer and a fashion trendsetter. When she arrives, sick and weak, it is Celie who nurses her back to health, prepares her meals, bathes her, and worships her. Celie soon comes to believe that she is in the presence of royalty whenever Shug Avery is around.

There is no doubt that Shug knows her way around, and holds small regard for public opinion, especially when it comes to her long-standing relationship with Mr. __. She offers no apology. Celie, in her state of naivete and innocence, finds herself in disbelief that a woman like Shug exists. Likewise, Shug is thunderstruck to encounter a woman so unknowing as Celie. Celie knows nothing about her body, views herself as ugly (as she's been told), rarely smiles, and has accepted, more or less, Mr. __'s brand of intimacy as a dispassionate assault she is, by fate, doomed to endure.

Despite Shug's long-standing affairs with Mr. __, she and Celie develop an affection with both a physical and an emotional dimension. Shug Avery, in Celie's estimation, is the "Queen Honeybee" (see *Color Purple* 40). When Celie begins to sew clothing for Shug—gowns for evening performances at Harpo's jookjoint, and simple dresses for day wear, she searches the dry goods store for purple fabric, so that Shug can be adorned in royal color. Ironically, if there is a "messenger of God" in Walker's novel, it is Shug Avery.

Shug, a sensual woman, is not above using her rapport with Albert (known as Mr. ___ to Celie) as a means of controlling his behavior toward Celie. Most important, Shug has access to Mr. ___'s personal items, and discovers a cache of letters, written by Nettie to Celie over many years, and hidden by Mr. ___. When Celie regains her equilibrium after reading the letters, her only wish is to take Mr. ___'s life; she dreams of slitting his throat. Knowing now that her sister is alive, living in Africa, she no longer writes to God, but to Nettie. Celie's two lost babies have, in fact, grown up under Nettie's loving care, with the missionary family.

Although Shug uncovers Nettie's letters, her greatest and most precious gift to Celie is an internal self-portrait. Shug is largely responsible for aiding Celie in self-discovery and teaching her about self-esteem; she even writes a song for her and sings it at Harpo's place. The tune is called "Miss Celie's Blues."[27] As Celie discovers more about herself and the world in which she lives, she begins to view both differently, reflecting, at Shug's urging, on her image of God, and finally replacing her own traditional image with the all-encompassing one offered by Shug.

As Celie's period of initiation continues, her sense of vulnerability begins to shrink, and her world enlarges. Mr. ___, nonetheless, persists in his usual mistreatment of Celie, when Shug, well enough to travel now, is not around. Ultimately, Shug calls a moratorium on Mr. ___'s physical abuse of Celie, who is all the more forthcoming toward womanhood and female power.

Celie's third and final stage of movement into womanhood and power is evidenced by what might be called sacred language, used in a profane situation.[28] The high moment of this third stage occurs at the dinner table in the home of Sofia's sister, Odessa, where the family is gathered—Harpo, Sofia, Odessa's husband, Jack, Shug, her new lover, Grady, Celie, and all the children. Dinner has been served, and the evening is winding down. Shug makes an announcement that precipitates Celie's show of preparedness for incorporation. Shug's announcement that Celie is leaving with her triggers bewilderment and then refusal in Mr. ___. Celie quickly joins the battle by calling Mr. ___ names, asking if he has received other letters from Nettie, and then drawing boldly on her own ancient female power, cursing him into the next life and back, promising him suffering all the way. Celie continues to rain curses upon Mr. ___ until Shug shakes her back into the present.

Celie, now having entered into the fullness of womanhood, uttering, speaking herself there by locating her authoritative voice, exercises her latent female power and is, then, incorporated into the sanctum of womanhood. Shug's shaking her brings Celie out of the trancelike state in which she experienced transformation.[29]

Celie, Shug, and Grady move to Memphis, and Celie begins to sew again, this time making pants of every size, shape, and color for her friends and family back home. Alone and lonely now, Mr. ___ is living under Celie's curse and incantations. He confines himself to the house, and lives every moment under the threat of nameless, shapeless fear—an unarticulated fear—scarcely sleeping, and taking food only by necessity. So great is his fear and trembling that the sound of his own heartbeat reverberates and becomes a thunderous noise under the darkness of a night sky.

Both Hurston and Walker use elements of the natural world to dramatize the strength and power their women appropriate. They signal the presence of female power through the use of symbols such as Walker's dust devil. Likewise, in *Jonah's Gourd Vine*, Hurston draws upon the same natural phenomena to add force to the import of Lucy's death, and John's subsequent fear:

> That night a wind arose about the house and blew from the kitchen wall to the clump of oleanders that screened the chicken house . . . and a pack of dogs followed it, howling, barking and whining until the break of day, and John huddled beneath his bed-covers shaking and afraid. (213)

As Hurston and Walker call the natural elements into vigorous play, they suggest that woman's power, too, is a natural emanation, and the universe explodes in response to her call—acknowledging and sanctifying this woman-power.

At the center of understanding the genesis of Hurston's and Walker's fictive woman in African-American communities, particularly those of the rural South, is understanding the concept of birth and rebirth of both a people and a constellation of ideas, myths, and actual historical events that both shape and provide cultural meaning. Culture *is* meaning. The benefits of this reflective culture are many. Important among them is the continuity such fiction as Hurston's and Walker's provides for the construction and reconstruction of a historical mode of thought. Thus, the images of these writers' Africa-descended women are filtered through a kaleidoscopic lens that encourages self-reflection, over time, to the present.

In *Jonah's Gourd Vine* and *The Color Purple*, Hurston and Walker depict the African-American woman's community as an enclosure—a vessel—in which the cycle of birth and rebirth incorporates the new and hallows the ancient.

NOTES

1. Not only were Hurston's and Walker's youths spent in neighboring states, but their parallel or collateral references to the natural elements that fill linear space—trees, flowers, water—and perceptual space, sacred ancestral worlds, and ritual behavior, such as An' Pheemy's, and the air that forms Celie's words as she curses Mr. ___, are resonances between these two novelists. For a discussion of the cultural geography of space, see Zelinsky.

2. During the Atlantic slave trade to the Americas, cultural diffusion, or the process by which culture traits or behaviors spread from one place to another, occurred between Florida, Hurston's natal state, and Walker's Georgia. Cultural diffusion includes storytelling styles, jokes, myths, and values assimilation. In the late seventeenth and early eighteenth centuries, slave ships landed at St. Augustine, Florida, and at a later period, Florida became a refuge for runaway slaves from Georgia and South Carolina. See Donnan.

An excellent definition of cultural diffusion is offered in Hunter and Whitten, *Encyclopedia of Anthropology* (126). Cultural diffusion occurs when different cultures come in contact over time with one another. Inevitably, there is some transfer of various significant beliefs and practices.

3. Many anthropologists use this term in reference to a fundamental set of beliefs about the world, shared by members of a group or community, as represented in their myths, lore, ceremonies, attitudes, and social behavior. This is also the essential definition of the term to which I subscribe (Robert H. Winthrop, *Dictionary of Concepts and Cultural Anthropology* 82–85).

4. Vulnerability and ancient African female power are terms that are, obviously, open to discussion, especially in contexts that differ from my own. In this essay the basis for these terms is an African worldview, as articulated by Ray: "African mythology explains the world by reference to symbolic oppositions and polarities that serve to categorize complex social and moral relationships" (37).

5. Bantu is one of four major languages spoken on the African continent, primarily in the Niger-Kongo area. The other language groupings are Nilo-Saharan; Khoisan, or Hottentot-Bushman; and African-Asiatic, or Hamitic-Semitic. See also Hunter and Whitten, 238–242.

6. As a result of the major European players in the slave trade to the Americas, English, as spoken in Europe, directly impacted slave English/dialects. See Herskovits.

7. An excellent source on African-American slave culture is Stuckey, *Slave Culture*, particularly the Introduction.

8. For further clarity of the concept "African female power," see Drewal and Drewal.

9. Hathor, or Isis/Hathor, the Great Mother deity of the Egyptians, includes Nut, the Sky Goddess. Neumann, in *The Great Mother*, states: "In reality the unity of Hathor, Nut and Isis encompasses all goddesses" (218). Indeed, these are the multiple manifestations of these goddesses, which include fertility, sacred cow, parthenogenetic goddess, moon goddess, Lady of the Sycamore tree, and other designations.

10. In Thompson, *Flash of the Spirit*, several discussions of female worship among the Yoruba of Brazil are furnished. For example, see Thompson on the riverine goddess, Yemoja (72). There is also reputed to be a community of African-Americans in South Carolina who have retained much of traditional Yoruba culture.

11. The "Great Mothers" of the southwestern Yoruba pantheon of gods and goddesses are recognized as gods. Through these women, the elderly and female ancestor spirits, the Yoruba pay homage to the female forces within the universe, as they believe that women possess unparalleled power (see Drewal and Drewal 7).

12. The Yoruba equate the bird with the human head, or the seat of power and knowledge. "A bird atop a healer's staff shows the Mothers how powerful the healer is with his herbs." As powerful female spirits, "owners of the birds," the Mothers own the knowledge of Yoruba society, and thus are deeply feared and revered (Drewal and Drewal 47).

13. Generally *ashe* may be considered as "the power to make things happen . . . or 'So be it; may it happen' " (Drewal and Drewal 5–7).

14. The Gelede Festival, performed in daylight, follows the Efe Night ceremony. These two performances—a *duality* of events—are inseparable; they also emphasize the fact that older women are seen as repositories of both good and evil potential. During the Gelede Festival the elderly women are accorded special place at the opening of the human circle from which the dancers and other performers enter the community. The entrance is known as "the mouth of authority." The majority of Gelede performers are male. All performers wear female attire, with emphasis given to protruding breasts and large buttocks, symbols of female fertility and the mystery of bringing forth new life.

15. Once again, the African concept of duality can be seen in the contrasting or oppositional forces—protection and malevolence—vested in the Mothers. Either term, the Great Mothers, or the Mothers, may be used interchangeably.

16. Given the wide distribution of Yoruba slaves in the New World, and the impact of cultural contact, and thus cultural diffusion, one could reasonably believe that African-diasporic blacks, the world over, remain very much affected by their cultural heritage. See, for example, Herskovits, *The Myth of the Negro Past*.

17. Hurston's and Walker's historical memory is frequently visible in the Africanisms they incorporate in much of their fiction. Utterances, or profound statements, come not only through their female characters, but from both sexes, where such characters assume a performance-related quality.

18. Hemenway suggests that Hurston attempts to "establish herself in a man's world" through "the communication context of the . . . courting scene between John and Lucy," in his "Are You a Flying Lark or a Setting Dove?" (Fisher and Stepto 133).

19. Western social science has attached a negative connotation to the term "matriarch," in that it suggests denigration of the black male by the black female. In the context used in this essay, however, the term refers to the senior woman in an African-American community, particularly in the early, rural South—a woman who is learned in herbal medicine, midwifery, healing rituals, and the like.

20. Edy and Della, obviously assistants to An' Pheemy, could "sweeten" or freshen and cleanse Lucy, but neither could perform the ritual functions handled by An' Pheemy, who held elevated social status in the community.

21. It is interesting to compare Hurston's An' Pheemy's ritual burial of the afterbirth under a tree, with a statement Celie makes in *The Color Purple* about turning into a tree when Mr. __ beats her (22).

22. Spiders have symbolic meaning in many cultures. For instance, in North Africa, the spider is a female, spinner of fate. See Barbara Walker 957.

23. Later in the novel, after Lucy's death, John and Hattie Tyson marry while he is still under the spell cast by An' Dangie DeWoe, with Tyson's encouragement and participation. The marriage, however, is doomed from the beginning.

24. Most Bantu-speaking African slaves in the New World, and doubtless their early descendants, consigned the elders to the spirit world, as they are closest to the ancestors. Even in current African society—such as among the peoples of the Niger-Kongo—there is thought to be a constant dialogue between the ancestral spirits and those still in the phenomenal world, or the land of the living. This dialogue is evidenced in many ways, such as in art, music, and ceremonies. The Gelede Festival among the Yoruba is replete with indications of the power vested in the elders. See also Thompson and Cornet, *The Four Moments of the Sun.*

25. The goddess Sofia "achieves her supreme visible form 'as a flower' "; and is, also, a unity of several other goddesses, including Isis (Neumann 325).

26. Arnold Van Gennep was born in 1873 and died in 1957. He was a pioneer in the field of ethnography, and is credited as the first to provide a means or framework for understanding transitions of individuals or groups within a society.

27. Alice Walker comments on "Miss Celie's Blues," sung in the movie by Shug to Celie: "I will never forget the moment the phone rang, and Quincy Jones announced on the other end that 'They (he, Rod Temperton and Lionel Richie) had it' " (notes from the score of the film version of Walker's *The Color Purple*)—meaning the theme song, the all-important song Shug sings to Celie in the jookjoint, the song in which Shug's love for Celie is first expressed.

28. Inferentially, Walker suggests, I believe, that Celie's outpouring of words comes from an internal, God-like source. Celie and Shug have discussed the "It" god, inside all humankind.

29. Celie's trancelike state is reminiscent of the "spirit" Hurston discusses in *Tell My Horse*, during which an individual is mounted by a "spirit-rider," or "loa." "Under the whip and guidance of the spirit-rider, the horse [person] does and says many things that she or he would never have uttered un-ridden" (*Tell My Horse* 234). The substantive difference in outcomes is that Celie's utterances are indicative of a permanent transformation of the self.

WORKS CITED

Baranouw, Victor. *Culture and Personality*. Homewood, Ill.: Dorsey Press, 1973.

Bell, Roseann, et al. *Sturdy Black Bridges: Visions of Black Women in Literature*. Garden City, N.Y.: Anchor Press/Doubleday, 1979.

Briffault, Robert. *The Mothers*. New York: Atheneum, 1977.

Budge, Wallis E. A. *Osiris and the Egyptian Resurrection*. Vols. 1 and 2. New York: Dover Publications, 1973.

Donnan, Elizabeth. *Documents Illustrative of the History of the Slave Trade to America.* Washington, D.C.: Carnegie Institute of Washington, 1935.

Drewal, Henry John, and Margaret Thompson Drewal. *Gelede*. Bloomington: Indiana University Press, 1983.

Fisher, Dexter, and Robert B. Stepto, eds. *Afro-American Literature: The Reconstruction of Instruction.* New York: Modern Language Association, 1979.
Franklin, John Hope. *From Slavery to Freedom: A History of the Negro Americans.* 4th ed. New York: Alfred A. Knopf, 1974.
Genovese, Eugene D. *Roll, Jordan, Roll: The World the Slaves Made.* New York: Pantheon Books, 1974.
Hart, George. *A Dictionary of Egyptian Gods and Goddesses.* New York: Routledge & Kegan Paul, 1986.
Herskovits, Melville J. *The Myth of the Negro Past.* Boston: Beacon Press, 1958.
Hughes, Langston, and Arna Bontemps, eds. *The Book of Negro Folklore.* New York: Dodd, Mead, 1958.
Hunter, David E., and Phillip Whitten. *Encyclopedia of Anthropology.* New York: Harper & Row, 1976.
Hurston, Zora Neale. *Jonah's Gourd Vine.* New York: J. B. Lippincott, 1934, 1971.
——. *Tell My Horse.* Philadelphia: J. B. Lippincott, 1938; Berkeley, Calif.: Turtle Island Press, 1981.
Kanter, Emanuel. *The Amazons.* Chicago: Charles H. Kerr, 1926.
Karanja, Ayana. "Speak Softly to Me in the Morning." Ph.D. diss., The Union Institute, Cincinnati, Ohio, 1981.
Levine, Lawrence W. *Black Culture and Black Consciousness.* New York: Oxford University Press, 1979.
Lévi-Strauss, Claude. *Myth and Meaning.* New York: Schocken Books, 1978.
Neumann, Erich. *The Great Mother.* Princeton, N.J.: Princeton University Press, 1963.
Pryse, Marjorie, and Hortense J. Spillers. *Conjuring: Black Women, Fiction, and Literary Tradition.* Bloomington: Indiana University Press, 1985.
Ray, Benjamin C. *African Religions: Symbol, Ritual and Community.* Englewood Cliffs, N.J.: Prentice-Hall, 1976.
Schure, Edouard. *The Great Initiates: The Study of the Secret History of Religions.* San Francisco: Harper & Row, 1961.
Seager, Joni, and Ann Olson. *Women in the World Atlas.* New York: Simon & Schuster, 1986.
Sheffey, Ruthe T., ed. *A Rainbow Round Her Shoulder.* Baltimore: Morgan State University Press, 1982.
Shweder, Richard A., and Robert A. Levine. *Culture Theory: Essays on Mind, Self, and Emotion.* New York: Cambridge University Press, 1984.
Stuckey, Sterling. *Slave Culture: Nationalist Theory and the Foundations of Black America.* New York: Oxford University Press, 1987.
Thompson, Robert Farris. *Flash of the Spirit: African and Afro-American Art and Philosophy.* New York: Vintage Books, 1984.
Thompson, Robert Farris, and Joseph Cornet. *The Four Moments of the Sun: Kongo Art in Two Worlds.* Washington, D.C.: National Gallery of Art, 1981.
Van Gennep, Arnold. *The Rites of Passage.* Chicago: University of Chicago Press, 1972.
Walker, Alice. *The Color Purple.* New York: Harcourt Brace Jovanovich, 1982.
Walker, Barbara G. *The Woman's Encyclopedia of Myths and Secrets.* San Francisco: Harper & Row, 1983.
Zelinsky, Wilbur. *The Cultural Geography of the United States.* Englewood Cliffs, N.J.: Prentice-Hall, 1973.

12

Benediction: A Few Words About *The Temple of My Familiar*, Variously Experienced, and *Possessing the Secret of Joy*

Lillie P. Howard

When I began this book years ago, actually began the physical task of pulling people together to see just what we could do about Zora and Alice, I wondered aloud about Walker's silences. Nudged on by the sporadic appearances of her "nature" essays and poems, amidst the jarring criticism of *The Color Purple*, I imagined her deep in her own wilderness, staring out at the life she had made for herself. She seemed to be retreating from people in order to get to know them better. Her profound and newly formed interest in animals and the universe could only heighten her keen interest in, and bring her back to, people. In essence, just as she had become most successful, she had become the least visible. While I asked aloud, "Just what is Alice doing?" I felt that I already knew. She was watching, listening, and waiting for her own true self to arrive and give her strength to continue to be.

When I later read *Living by the Word*, which put me in touch with the seeking Alice in ways that none of her works had before, I was surprised to see just how much she really had rested in order better to gauge her own restlessness. I also saw how troubled she had been by the reception of *The Color Purple*—both the prizes it garnered and the strident criticism—and how much she had sought the answers to her own questions within herself.

It seemed clear that she had not been working on *Olive Oil*, a promise of old, but that she had been working on herself—enlarging her soul and psyche to include all of her ancestors, including the old white man who, by raping her great-great-grandmother, became Alice's great-great-grandfather.

In essence, she had done for herself what she said (in "Good Night, Willie Lee, I'll See You in the Morning") Zora, Nella Larsen, and Jean Toomer, had at one point in their lives, done for themselves—retreated from writing in order to find that from which writing derives its meaning: life itself. Her contemplation of life took her back through the ages and gave her the visions she unfolds in *The Temple of My Familiar* (1988) and *Possessing the Secret of Joy* (1992).

~

Before Walker published *The Temple of My Familiar*, she unleashed it, almost chapter by chapter, in whatever magazine was quick enough to grab it. Thus *The Temple* unfolded gradually in *New Woman*, *Essence*, *Lear's*, and elsewhere. For those who could not wait for the real thing, reading the *Temple* that way, bit by bit, must have been maddening. Indeed, the book is maddening even if one starts at the beginning and reads straight through. To care for it at all, one has to suspend almost everything one has studiously and conscientiously accepted about novels—their form, purpose, structure, and so on—and simply experience, if one dares, page upon page of the work. Walker's own restrictions about citing excerpts from her works encourage this approach.

At first I wondered not so much about the novel but about Walker herself, living off in the woods some place in California, talking about horses, trees, and the like, not unlike Zora Neale Hurston, who also retired from life as she had known it, finding it less painful to talk about cheese with holes, the man in the moon, and other compelling topics. After a cursory reading of a few pages of *Temple*, I immediately thought that Alice had been away too long, that she had made a mistake by moving so far away from the people she had so earnestly written about. Somehow, she had become "terched" (i.e., touched in the head); her characters were "terched," especially Lissie of *Temple*. It seemed safer to put the book aside rather than to subject myself to it. Perhaps, in time, the inclination to read it would simply pass.

What I discovered by persevering (for the sake of *this* book), however, is that *The Temple* has a rhythm of its own and that if given half a chance, the current (for the beat is continuous, relentless) of that rhythm carries the reader along with it to unwashed shores. Having discovered that, I decided to let Alice Walker have her way and just hang on as best I could, content simply to capture my own experiences as I came in touch with the experiences of the book. As the novel "called," I responded.

Having heard Alice Walker speak, I know that it is her voice I hear when reading *The Temple of My Familiar*. The voice is clear, gravely matter-of-fact, telling again a story she has often told, of despair, disconnectedness, disenchantment, the suspension of people between centuries and cultures, between life and nonlife—and all this within the first five pages of the novel. As Walker "roams through the ages," she lets centuries of stories tell themselves through the medium of her voice.

The Temple is about everyone and everything, then, almost since the beginning of time, including this time. Its movement flings one back and forth across millennia, continents, physical and spiritual wastelands sometimes inhabited by people bereft of themselves, unaware of and afraid of their essence. The result is mental and physical disorientation, heightened by the fact that one's movement, both horizontally and vertically, occurs within a world where plant becomes animal, animal human, the cycle repeating itself continuously. In fact, everything is personified as the reader is bandied back and forth between the worlds of Lissie's many lives and the past that formed Zede. Suwelo, one of the book's main characters, seems to be a modern-day and a latter-day Truman Held (from Walker's *Meridian*) who has been separated from his "present" in order more fully to experience and appreciate his past. His "cabin" is the row house in Baltimore left to him by his Uncle Rafe. His privilege and penance is to spend significant time with his ancestors, Hal and Miss Lissie, in order to anchor his past within theirs and thereby make his present meaningful.

Strangely, "the temple of my familiar," which appears without warning in one of the stories, is a live "pet," part bird, part fish, and part reptile. Though immortal, persevering, in spite of efforts to kill him off—like African-American culture and history in general—the "temple's" story is an unwelcome distraction. Walker seems to think it important that the pet's story be known, however, for in his story lies something of our own. It is up to the reader, then, to generate the interest and the patience needed to establish kinship.

Some of the most wondrous passages in the book appear on pages 170, 173, and 186, for it is here that Walker reiterates the theme of her poem "Fundamental Difference" (from *Revolutionary Petunias*), and reaffirms Meridian's declaration (in Walker's novel of the same name) that the songs of the people must never be lost. Instead, they must be passed from generation to generation, transformed by the experiences of each. The songs are represented here by the "humming," which has as much meaning as singing; it is guttural, primordial, the "key" that unlocks for Fanny the mystery and the source of her being.

These passages speak a language many will understand; they strike dormant chords inside the deep passages of ourselves. Like the keys they metaphorize, they open us up to ourselves and the wonders of those selves, and they send us searching, like the bits of sand in Hurston's *Their Eyes Were Watching God*, for the others who are, who must be, like us, though perhaps they do not yet have the keys or even know that they exist. The past, then, is enormously important, for only by knowing the past can one have a meaningful present.

Because the book's characters are so ill-prepared to deal with their present, rarely are they allowed the luxury of one. Rather, they spend the majority of their time existing either in a surreal dreamlike state (e.g., Fanny and Carlotta, throughout most of the novel) or they are the hosts of lengthy flashbacks (e.g., Miss Lissie) into the past. All this contributes to an atmospheric eeriness that is only pierced by all the talking going on. That is, the novel often plunges its characters and its readers into darkness, thereby sharpening their hearing, so that they can listen all the better to the stories they need to hear. In a way reminiscent of the African oral tradition, we must gather round to receive, from those who have gone before, the wisdom of the ages.

In technique and atmosphere, *The Temple* resembles a modern epic where the main characters journey to a faraway place that turns out to be themselves—their past, present, and future, all rolled together. To achieve wholeness, they each must journey back through the past to pick up (i.e., retrieve) those pieces of themselves that they have lost. Once they have found them, they will experience their own "humming."

The book's stories are woven like pieces of a "many lives" quilt, each connected to the other though the thread is sometimes thin, broken, invisible. Still, one values the whole because of its parts, imperfectly woven, imperfectly lived, imperfectly understood.

Given the book's handling or "mishandling" of time and place and technique, its displacement of characters and reader, one would be hard-pressed to call *The Temple* a novel, for, like Jean Toomer's *Cane*, it is not that. Rather, it transcends that form, defying description and categorization. It is a history, stretched out through eternity and yet boiled down to a drop of now, which can, at best, only hint at an essence that must be experienced repeatedly, layer upon layer, at a dizzying pace, to be fully realized.

When I finished reading Walker's *Temple*, I felt as though I had barely begun. The work defies full explanation because it is meant to be experienced, without judgment, rather than explained or rendered anew. The reader is encouraged to connect with the book, its characters and messages, on any and every plane, at every sensory level; and each reader is encouraged to find his or her own way, his or her own "key" to unlock the mysteries of the book, the past: "The humming has started inside. I gots my own humming now, hooking up with the humming of the various characters in the book. And what a mighty chorus we be."

~

On the heels of *The Temple* came the novel that may supplant *The Color Purple* as Walker's most compelling and controversial book. If one had to put the *Temple* aside every few chapters in order to orient one's self, one has to put *Possessing the Secret of Joy* aside in order to still the indescribable wretchedness the book engenders in one's own body and mind and spirit.

In the Foreword to Brian Lanker and Barbara Summers's *I Dream a World*, Maya Angelou reminds us:

> Black women whose ancestors were brought to the United States beginning in 1619 have lived through conditions of cruelties so horrible, so bizarre, the women had to re-invent themselves. They had to find safety and sanctity inside themselves or they would not have been able to tolerate those tortuous lives. They had to learn to be self-forgiving quickly, for often their exterior exploits were at odds with their interior beliefs. (Angelou 8)

"Lives lived in such cauldrons," continues Angelou, "are either obliterated or forged into impenetrable alloys." Walker presents to us in *Possessing the Secret of Joy* a cauldron of our own making (none of us is innocent, she makes clear), and allows us to see inside an alloy forged out of a horror almost too painful to imagine, much less bear. And yet, Walker wants the world to know that this horror is borne every day by millions of women and has been borne for unspeakable centuries. One does not want to read *Possessing the Secret of Joy*. Instead, clutching one's stomach as the pain pierces up from the womb, one wants to howl to the winds and the heavens in angry protest and despair.

Possessing the Secret of Joy is a multivoiced story of the ancient African Olinka tradition of female circumcision. Simultaneously gripping and repelling, the book is written with a mission in mind: "I have one requirement," said Walker in a 1992 interview in *Essence*, "that because of this book, one little girl won't be mutilated" (58).

While one has no trouble comprehending the atrocities the novel unveils, the book is difficult to read nonetheless without experiencing physical, mental, and emotional outrage. In Walker's first novel, *The Third Life of Grange Copeland*, we learned that while the atrocities whites had visited upon blacks were legion, they were neither mask nor excuse for the historical and everyday pain blacks often visit upon one another, Walker offering us Grange Copeland and his kin as prime examples.

Possessing the Secret of Joy picks up Tashi, a character from *The Color Purple* and *The Temple of My Familiar*. In tight, sometimes staccato chapters, the book slowly, painfully unfolds her story of genital mutilation. This mutilation has years before killed Tashi's sister and countless others and has left "one hundred million" other women of African, Asian, and Arab descent walking with a "familiar" shuffle that recalls both their past and present. The novel sends a silent but piercing cry to the universe immediately to ban this ancient initiation rite so that "no other little girl will be so mutilated."

The novel is not one for the timid, then, for its message is raw, stark, meant to make the reader both experience and excise the pain, and to justify the methodical madness that Tashi (wife to Adam, Celie's son—see *The Color Purple*; also known as Evelyn and Tashi-Evelyn) embraces and from the depths of which she lucidly recounts her own ascent, including her revenge against M'Lissa.

M'Lissa, the African midwife, has become a national monument because of her unusual contribution to her society—that of casually removing with very crude and unsanitary tools (such as sharpened rocks) all or part of the clitoris of little African girls, and then sewing them up so tightly that neither urine nor menstrual blood can flow easily out of their bodies. This practice was thought to make females more feminine, since the clitoris was thought to be like the male penis. All of this was done, of course, without anesthesia or sterilization, for the express pleasure of African men, many of whom enjoyed splitting open their brides on their wedding night "like a watermelon." Childbirth under these conditions was an unspeakable agony, leaving Tashi and Adam, who marvelled over their son's birth as an immaculate conception since Adam was not able to penetrate Tashi, with a deformed child.

When Walker learned of the hideous practice of genital mutilation, she was outraged and felt that she had to speak out. When asked in the *Essence* interview what gave her, a Westerner, the right to intervene in African affairs, Walker responded:

> Slavery intervened. As far as I'm concerned, I am speaking for my great-great-great grandmother who came here with all this pain in her body. Think about it. In addition to having been captured, put in the hull of a ship, packed like sardines, put on the auction block, in addition to her children being sold, she being raped, in addition to all of this, she might have been genitally mutilated. I can't stand it! I would go nuts if this part of her story weren't factored in. Imagine

> if men came from Africa with their penises removed. Believe me, we would have many a tale about it. (102)

For the most part, the women of the Olinka society suffer in silence, for like most initiation rites, this one of genital circumcision is a profound secret, seeping through the lives of dazed women for whom sex is a nightmare and death welcome relief. The act is made even more horrible because it is visited upon women by other women—their mothers the collaborators, the midwife the instrument—all in the name of preserving a culture that has already denied them life. And yet, says Walker in the *Essence* interview, "It has been extremely difficult to blame our mothers for anything, because we can see so clearly what they've been up against. . . . How do you criticize someone who has 'made a way out of no way' for you?" But, continues Walker, "We have to. For our own health, we have to examine the ways in which we've been harmed by our mothers' collaboration" (62, 102).

Rather than blame her mother, Tashi-Evelyn seeks out the midwife, M'Lissa, who has by now become a virtual icon, accorded government privilege and heroine status, and kills her. To Tashi, the death is reparation for her own sister, who did not survive M'Lissa's blunt instruments, and for the mutilation and killing of the spirit she has visited for decades upon many, many women. For her "crime against society," Tashi-Evelyn is tried and imprisoned. None of this seems to matter to her, however, for her life has long been over. She has been living in the past, retrieving its meaning, and then using that to spur her on to the single purpose of what remains of her life—retribution.

In many ways, the terrible secret that the novel unlocks is also the secret that Tashi, through a series of flashbacks, must also unlock. In essence, she must recognize, acknowledge, and confront the thing that has driven her mad. Once she does, she is at peace.

Her comfort mirrors that of Walker herself, who told the *Essence* interviewer that she had

> never had a better time—weeping all the way, you know what I mean? You know the expression "unspeakable joy"? I have unspeakable joy even as I deal with my anger, sorrow, and grief. I don't have a big plan, a big scheme about all this. I have one requirement: that, because of this book, one little girl, somewhere, won't be mutilated. And that's plenty. That'll keep me laughing. I'll go home, I'll kick up my heels, and I'll feel that on this issue I've saved one child. That's enough. (102)

And so it is.

~

When I began this book, I wanted to show commonalities between Alice Walker and her foremother, Zora Neale Hurston. Those commonalities exist, and are ably pointed out by the book's contributors. Beyond those, however, in the here and now, thirty-plus years after the death of Zora Neale Hurston, we are left with Alice Walker herself, still drawing upon the past and the works of Hurston but going beyond all that to carve out a path uniquely her own. In many ways, like Zora, she remains as alone as ever. Again, like Zora, however, she does not care much about that, feeling that ultimately she only has to answer to herself.

If Zora were still alive today, she would probably consider Alice a kindred soul but keep her speaking distance. Were she to read Walker's novels, she would find much of herself within them, but might find the atmosphere a little straining and depressing. She would want a breath of fresh air. At the same time, she would not shy away from the truths rendered in Alice's fiction, for as she wrote in her autobiography, she knew "from hard searching . . . that tears and laughter, love and hate make up the sum of life" (348). Were the two authors to ever meet, perhaps at a "barbeque," they would like and complement each other: Zora would be prancing around telling stories to make people laugh, and Alice would be watching in wondrous silence, "possessing the secret of joy."

Selected Bibliography

Abrahams, Robert D. *Deep Down in the Jungle: Negro Narrative Folklore from the Streets of Philadelphia.* Chicago: Aldine, 1970.

Angelou, Maya. Foreword, *I Dream a World.* Edited by Brian Lanker and Barbara Summers. New York: Stewart, Tabori and Chang, 1989.

Banks, Erma Davis, and Keith Byerman. *Alice Walker: An Annotated Bibliography*. New York: Garland Publishing, 1989.

Baranouw, Victor. *Culture and Personality*. Homewood, Ill.: Dorsey Press, 1973.

Bell, Roseann, et al. *Sturdy Black Bridges: Visions of Black Women in Literature*. Garden City, N.Y.: Anchor Press/Doubleday, 1979.

Bethel, Lorraine. "This Infinity of Conscious Pain: Zora Neale Hurston and the Black Female Literary Tradition." In *But Some of Us Are Brave*, edited by Gloria T. Hull et al., 176–188. New York: Feminist Press, 1982.

Bone, Robert. *Down Home*. New York: G. P. Putnam's Sons, 1975.

Bradley, David. "Novelist Alice Walker: Telling the Black Woman's Story." *The New York Times Magazine*, January 8, 1984, pp. 25–37.

Braxton, Joanne, and Andree Nicola McLaughlin. *Wild Women in the Whirlwind: Afro-American Culture and the Contemporary Literature Renaissance*. New Brunswick, N.J.: Rutgers University Press, 1990.

Briffault, Robert. *The Mothers*. New York: Atheneum, 1977.

Brown, Lloyd W. "Zora Neale Hurston and the Nature of Female Perception." *Obsidian* 4, no. 3 (1978): 39–45.

Budge, Wallis E. A. *Osiris and the Egyptian Resurrection*. Vols. 1 and 2. New York: Dover Publications, 1973.

Byerman, Keith E. *Fingering the Jagged Grain: Tradition and Form in Recent Black Fiction.* Athens: University of Georgia Press, 1985.

Christian, Barbara. "Alice Walker." In *Dictionary of Literary Biography: Afro-American Fiction Writers After 1955*, vol. 33, edited by Thadious M. Davis and Trudier Harris, 258–271. Detroit: Buccoli Clark Layman, 1984.

———. "Alice Walker: The Black Woman Artist as Wayward." In *Black Women Writers (1950–1980): A Critical Evaluation*, edited by Mari Evans, 457–477. Garden City, N.Y.: Anchor Press/Doubleday, 1984.

———. *Black Women Novelists: The Development of a Tradition, 1892–1976*. Westport, Conn.: Greenwood Press, 1980.

———. "Trajectories of Self-Definition: Placing Contemporary Afro-American Women's Fiction." In *Black Feminist Criticism: Perspectives on Black Women Writers*, edited by Barbara Christian, 171–186. New York: Pergamon Press, 1985.

Davis, Thadious. "Alice Walker." In *Dictionary of Literary Biography: American Novelists Since World War II*, vol. 6, edited by James E. Kibler, Jr., 350–358. Detroit : Buccoli Clark Layman, 1980.

De Veaux, Alexis. "Alice Walker." *Essence Magazine* 20, no. 5 (September 1989): 56–58, 120–124.

Dixon, Melvin. *Ride Out the Wilderness: Geography and Identity in Afro-American Literature*. Urbana: University of Illinois Press, 1987.

Donnan, Elizabeth. *Documents Illustrative of the History of the Slave Trade to America*. Washington, D.C.: Carnegie Institute of Washington, 1935.

Drewal, Henry John, and Margaret Thompson Drewal. *Gelede*. Bloomington: Indiana University Press, 1983.

Ellison, Ralph. *Shadow and Act*. New York: Vintage Books, 1972.

Emerson, Ralph Waldo. *The Early Lectures of Ralph Waldo Emerson, 1838–1842*. Vol. 3. Edited by Robert E. Spiller and Wallace E. Williams. Cambridge, Mass.: Harvard University Press, 1972.

———. *Nature: Addresses and Lectures*. Boston: Houghton-Mifflin, 1903; New York: AMS Press, 1968.

Evans, Mari, ed. *Black Women Writers: Argument and Interviews*. London: Pluto Press, 1985.

——— *Black Women Writers (1950–1980): A Critical Evaluation*. Garden City, N.Y.: Anchor Press/Doubleday, 1984.

Fisher, Dexter, and Robert B. Stepto, eds. *Afro-American Literature: The Reconstruction of Instruction*. New York: Modern Language Association, 1979.

Franklin, John Hope. *From Slavery to Freedom: A History of the Negro Americans*. 4th ed. New York: Alfred A. Knopf, 1974.

Gates, Henry Louis, Jr. *Reading Black, Reading Feminist*. New York: Meridian Books, 1990.

———. *The Signifying Monkey*. New York: Oxford University Press, 1985.

Gayle, Addison, Jr. "The Outsider." In *Zora Neale Hurston*, Modern Critical Views, edited by Harold Bloom, 35–46. New York: Chelsea House, 1986.

———. *The Way of the New World*. New York: Doubleday, 1975.

Genovese, Eugene D. *Roll, Jordan, Roll: The World the Slaves Made*. New York: Pantheon Books, 1974.

Gilligan, Carol. *In Another Voice: Psychological Theory and Women's Development*. Cambridge, Mass.: Harvard University Press, 1982.

Gilligan, Carol, and Grant Wiggins. "The Origins of Morality in Early Childhood Relationships." Paper presented at the University of North Carolina at Chapel Hill, October 25, 1986.

Harris, Trudier. "Three Black Women Writers and Humanism: A Folk Perspective." In *Black American Literature and Humanism*, edited by R. Baxter Miller, 50–74. Lexington: University Press of Kentucky, 1981.

Hart, George. *A Dictionary of Egyptian Gods and Goddesses*. New York: Routledge & Kegan Paul, 1986.

Hemenway, Robert E. *Zora Neale Hurston: A Literary Biography*. Urbana: University of Illinois Press, 1977.

Hernton, Calvin. *The Sexual Mountain and Black Women Writers*. New York: Anchor Press, 1987.

Herskovits, Melville J. *The Myth of the Negro Past*. Boston: Beacon Press, 1958.

Howard, Lillie P. *Zora Neale Hurston*. Boston: Twayne, 1980.

Hughes, Langston, and Arna Bontemps, eds. *The Book of Negro Folklore*. New York: Dodd, Mead, 1958, 1983.

Hunter, David E., and Phillip Whitten. *Encyclopedia of Anthropology*. New York: Harper & Row, 1976.

Hurston, Zora Neale. *Dust Tracks on a Road: An Autobiography*. Philadelphia: J. B. Lippincott, 1942; Urbana: University of Illinois Press, 1971, 1984.

——. *Jonah's Gourd Vine*. Philadelphia: J. B. Lippincott, 1934, 1971.

——. *Moses, Man of the Mountain*. Philadelphia: J. B. Lippincott, 1939; Urbana: University of Illinois Press, 1984.

——. *Mules and Men*. Philadelphia: J. B. Lippincott, 1935; Bloomington: Indiana University Press, 1963, 1978.

——. *The Sanctified Church*. Berkeley, Calif.: Turtle Island Press, 1981.

——. *Seraph on the Suwanee*. New York: Charles Scribner & Sons, 1948.

——. *Tell My Horse*. Philadelphia: J. B. Lippincott, 1938; Berkeley, Calif.: Turtle Island Press, 1981.

——. *Their Eyes Were Watching God*. Philadelphia: J. B. Lippincott, 1937; Urbana: University of Illinois Press, 1978.

Kanter, Emanuel. *The Amazons*. Chicago: Charles H. Kerr, 1926.

Karanja, Ayana. "Speak Softly to Me in the Morning." Ph.D. diss., The Union Institute, Cincinnati, Ohio, 1981.

Karl, Frederick R. *American Fictions 1940–1980: A Comprehensive History and Critical Evaluation*. New York: Harper & Row, 1983.

Levine, Lawrence W. *Black Culture and Black Consciousness*. New York: Oxford University Press, 1979.

Lévi-Strauss, Claude. *Myth and Meaning*. New York: Schocken Books, 1978.

Meese, Elizabeth A. *Crossing the Double Cross: The Practice of Feminist Criticism*. Chapel Hill: University of North Carolina Press, 1986.

Neumann, Erich. *The Great Mother*. Princeton, N.J.: Princeton University Press, 1963.

Newton, Judith, and Deborah Rosenfelt, eds. *Feminist Criticism and Social Change: Sex, Class and Race in Literature and Culture*. New York: Methuen, 1985.

O'Brien, John, ed. *Interviews with Black Writers*. New York: Liveright, 1973.

Parker-Smith, Bettye J. "Alice Walker's Women: In Search of Some Peace of Mind." In *Black Women Writers (1950–1980): A Critical Evaluation*, edited by Mari Evans, 478–493. Garden City, N.Y.: Anchor Press/Doubleday, 1984.

Pryse, Marjorie, and Hortense J. Spillers. *Conjuring: Black Women, Fiction, and Literary Tradition*. Bloomington: Indiana University Press, 1985.

Ray, Benjamin C. *African Religions: Symbol, Ritual and Community*. Englewood Cliffs, N.J.: Prentice-Hall, 1976.

Rosenblatt, Roger. *Black Fiction*. Cambridge, Mass.: Harvard University Press, 1974.

Royster, Beatrice Horn. "The Ironic Vision of Four Black Women Novelists: A Study of the Novels of Jessie Fauset, Nella Larsen, Zora Neale Hurston, and Ann Petry." Ph.D. diss., Emory University, 1975.

Schure, Edouard. *The Great Initiates: The Study of the Secret History of Religions*. San Francisco: Harper & Row, 1961.

Seager, Joni, and Ann Olson. *Women in the World Atlas*. New York: Simon & Schuster, 1986.

Sheffey, Ruthe T., ed. *A Rainbow Round Her Shoulder*. Baltimore: Morgan State University Press, 1982.

Shweder, Richard A., and Robert A. Levine. *Culture Theory: Essays on Mind, Self, and Emotion*. New York: Cambridge University Press, 1984.

Spillers, Hortense, and Marjorie Pryse. *Conjuring: Black Women, Fiction, and Literary Tradition*. Bloomington: Indiana University Press, 1985.

Steinem, Gloria. "Do You Know This Woman: She Knows You: A Profile of Alice Walker." *Ms.*, 10 (June 1982): 35–37, 89–92.

Stepto, Robert B. *From Behind the Veil: A Study of Afro-American Narrative*. Urbana: University of Illinois Press, 1979.

Stevens, Anthony. *Archetypes: A Natural History of the Self*. New York: William Morrow, 1982.

Stuckey, Sterling. *Slave Culture: Nationalist Theory and the Foundations of Black America*. New York: Oxford University Press, 1987.

Tate, Claudia. "Alice Walker." In *Black Women Writers at Work*, edited by Claudia Tate, 175–187. New York: Continuum, 1984.

Thompson, Robert Farris. *Flash of the Spirit: African and Afro-American Art and Philosophy*. New York: Vintage Books, 1984.

Thompson, Robert Farris, and Joseph Cornet. *The Four Moments of the Sun: Kongo Art in Two Worlds*. Washington, D.C.: National Gallery of Art, 1981.

Van Gennep, Arnold. *The Rites of Passage*. Chicago: University of Chicago Press, 1972.

Wade-Gayles, Gloria. "Anatomy of an Error: *The Color Purple* Controversy." *Catalyst*, premiere issue, 1986, 50–53.

Walker, Alice. *The Color Purple*. New York: Harcourt Brace Jovanovich, 1982; New York: Washington Square Press, 1982.

———. *Her Blue Body Everything We Know: Earthling Poems, 1965–1990*. New York: Harcourt Brace Jovanovich, 1991.

———. *Horses Make a Landscape Look More Beautiful: Poems*. New York: Harcourt Brace Jovanovich, 1984.

———. *I Love Myself When I Am Laughing . . . and Then Again When I Am Looking Mean and Impressive: A Zora Neale Hurston Reader*. New York: Feminist Press, 1979.

———. *In Love and Trouble: Stories of Black Women*. New York: Harcourt, Brace, 1973.

———. "In Search of Our Mothers' Gardens." *Ms.* (May 1974).

———. *In Search of Our Mothers' Gardens: Womanist Prose*. New York: Harcourt Brace Jovanovich, 1983.

———. Interview with Paula Giddings. *Essence* 23, no. 3 (July 1992): 59–60, 62, 102.

——. *Living by the Word: Selected Writings—1973–1987*. New York: Harcourt Brace Jovanovich, 1988.

——. *Meridian*. New York: Harcourt, Brace, 1976; New York: Pocket Books/Simon & Schuster, 1976.

——. *Once: Poems*. New York: Harcourt, Brace, 1968.

——. Personal statement/portrait. In *I Dream a World*, edited by Brian Lanker and Barbara Summers. New York: Stewart, Tabori, and Chang, 1989.

——. *Possessing the Secret of Joy*. New York: Harcourt Brace Jovanovich, 1992.

——. *Revolutionary Petunias and Other Poems*. New York: Harcourt, Brace, 1973.

——. *The Temple of My Familiar*. New York: Harcourt Brace Jovanovich, 1988.

——. *The Third Life of Grange Copeland*. New York: Harcourt, Brace, 1970.

Walker, Barbara G. *The Woman's Encyclopedia of Myths and Secrets*. San Francisco: Harper & Row, 1983.

Washington, Mary Helen. "An Essay on Alice Walker." In *Sturdy Black Bridges: Visions of Black Women in Literature*, edited by Roseann Bell et. al., 133–149. Garden City, N.Y.: Anchor Press/Doubleday, 1979.

Willis, Susan. *Specifying: Black Women Writing the American Experience*. Madison: University of Wisconsin Press, 1987.

Winthrop, Robert H. *Dictionary of Concepts and Cultural Anthropology*. Westport, Conn.: Greenwood Press, 1991.

Zelinsky, Wilbur. *The Cultural Geography of the United States*. Englewood Cliffs, N.J.: Prentice-Hall, 1973.

Index

About the Contributors

VALERIE BABB, Associate Professor of English at Georgetown University, is the author of several articles and two other books, *Ernest Gaines* and *Black Georgetown Remembered: A History of Its Black Community from the Founding of the "Town of George" in 1751 to the Present Day.*

JOANNE CORNWELL is Associate Professor of French and African-American studies in the departments of French and Africana Studies at San Diego State University. Professor Cornwell's research and publication focuses on African and African diaspora literatures. She is currently working on a volume of critical essays of African women writers.

EMMA J. WATERS DAWSON has studied, taught, and published on the works of various African-American authors, including Zora Neale Hurston, Jean Toomer, Alice Walker, Gwendolyn Brooks, and Toni Morrison, in *Obsidian*, *The Ronald McNair Journal*, and *The Aching Hearth* (1991). She is currently collaborating on the forthcoming book *Toni Morrison: A Bio-Bibliography*, to be published by Greenwood Press.

ALICE FANNIN teaches in the English Department and is an affiliate in Women's Studies at Miami University. Besides the publication "Psychic Survival" on Zora Neale Hurston and Alice Walker, she has published an article on poetry for children by African-American poets Lucille Clifton, Mari Evans, and Nikki Giovanni in *The Children's Literature Association Journal* (Summer 1981) and co-edited a women's literature anthology, *Woman: An Affirmation* (1979).

TRUDIER HARRIS is J. Carlyle Sitterson Professor of English at the University of North Carolina at Chapel Hill, where she has taught courses in African-American literature and folklore since she joined the faculty in 1979. Author, editor, and co-editor of eleven volumes, her most recent scholarly work is *Fiction and Folklore: The Novels of Toni Morrison* (1991). She is currently one of the three editors for the forthcoming *Oxford Companion to African-American Literature*.

LILLIE P. HOWARD, the editor of this volume, is Professor of English and Associate Vice President for Academic Affairs at Wright State University, Dayton, Ohio. In addition to writing her dissertation on Zora Neale Hurston and publishing a volume on Hurston (1980), Howard has published numerous articles on African-American literature.

AYANA KARANJA is Director of the African-American Studies Program at Loyola University, Chicago, where she also teaches courses in anthropology and African-American literature. She is the author of a full-length dialogic, mythopoetic manuscript on the life of Zora Neale Hurston, and has given numerous presentations on her work.

MARY L. NAVARRO is Professor of English and Director of Honors at Sinclair Community College, Dayton, Ohio. A teacher of women's literature and honors English, she actively works to create professional development opportunities for women in two-year colleges. She has presented papers on Toni Morrison, Alice Walker, women collaborating, and, most recently, on *Thelma and Louise*. Mary and Bianca, her cat, mutually share their solitude.

MARY H. SIMS has published a study on Anne Sexton and presented papers on Alice Walker, Toni Morrison, and Phillis Wheatley. A poet of sorts, she reads with the Silvery Moon Poets in Muncie and other places. Her poems have appeared in *Nausea Is the Square Root of Muncie*. As an artist, she refuses to throw the genius of Alice Walker away. Her paper *The Artistic Growth of Alice Walker: A Feminist Perspective* and her forthcoming dissertation, *From Harlem to Poontang Street: Sex and Sexuality in Alice Walker's "The Third Life of Grange Copeland,"* serve as testament to Mary's conviction and as witness to the future.

ANN FOLWELL STANFORD is Assistant Professor at the School for New Learning, DePaul University. She has published articles on Gwendolyn Brooks, Toni Cade Bambara, and Ralph Ellison, as well as studies of medical narrative. She is currently working on the connection between world illness and the body in African-American women's fiction.

ALICE WALKER, internationally known poet, essayist, and novelist, is the author of seventeen volumes, including the Pulitzer-Prize winning novel *The Color Purple*, an edited volume of Hurston works, *I Love Myself When I Am Laughing . . . and Then Again When I Am Looking Mean and Impressive: A Zora Neale Hurston Reader* (1979), and her latest compelling novel, *Possessing the Secret of Joy* (1992).

MARY ANN WILSON teaches a course on images of women in literature at the University of Southwestern Louisiana in Lafayette. She has published on other women writers such as Joyce Carol Oates and Carson McCullers, and has recently received a Louisiana Endowment for the Humanities grant to teach a summer institute on "Growing Up Female: Where Psychological Theory and Literary Text Meet." She is also at work on a study of the short fiction of Jean Stafford.

ISBN 0-313-25790-6
90000>
EAN
9 780313 257902
HARDCOVER BAR CODE